"*What Is Biblical Theology?* confirms Jim Hamilton's reputation as a top-shelf thinker and a wickedly good writer. This slim volume builds on the presupposition that the capacious biblical narrative—sixty-six books written by numerous authors and including stories, poems, proverbs, letters, and apocalypses—possesses a deep inner unity. Its unity arises from its divine inspiration, and it is in fact the true story of the whole world. Hamilton teaches his readers to engage in biblical theology, allowing the biblical story to shape us and conform us to God's will."

Bruce Riley Ashford, Provost, Dean of Faculty, and
Associate Professor of Theology and Culture, Southeastern Baptist
Theological Seminary

"*Theology* is a word that comes with baggage. Most people, like me, find their brains shutting down a little at its mention, mainly because it stirs up the same sort of feelings as words like *calculus* and *dentist appointment*. But from the outset of this book James Hamilton assures us he's not performing mental acrobatics (though I'm sure he could if he wanted to). Rather, he's showing us that if the Bible is a story, and God is a storyteller, then biblical theology is less like math and more like literature; it's less like a cold study of the chemical properties of paint and more like gazing at a Van Gogh. This is a book I wish I could have read a long time ago."

Andrew Peterson, singer/songwriter; author, *The Wingfeather Saga*

"This short, accessible book shows how we can move away from making the Bible all about us, reducing it to just another self-help book. Anyone who reads *What Is Biblical Theology?* will begin to discover what the Bible is really about and will have more 'Now I get it!' experiences as it equips readers to trace the thematic threads and story-line resolutions of the Bible from beginning to end."

Nancy Guthrie, author, *Seeing Jesus in the Old Testament* Bible study
series

"Disoriented Bible reading leads to disoriented living. Too often the Bible reader parachutes into a passage without understanding the immediate context or the overarching context of the entire Bible. Getting oriented to the whole story of the Bible is the only way to right interpretation and right living. Gaining this whole-Bible interpretive perspective is the burden of biblical theology, and Jim Hamilton has given us an outstanding introduction to this important yet neglected discipline. If the interpretive approach of Hamilton's book is applied, the reader will be able to better understand God's Word, know the mind of Christ, and glorify God."

K. Erik Thoennes, Professor of Theology, Chair, Talbot School of
Theology, Biola University; Pastor, Grace Evangelical Free Church,
La Mirada, California

"It is always a delight to read a book written by someone saturated in Scripture. This is one of those books."

Douglas Wilson, Senior Fellow of Theology, New St. Andrews College; Pastor, Christ Church, Moscow, Idaho

"It is an exciting privilege to watch and benefit from 'the coming of age' of the discipline of biblical theology in our generation. But in the explosion of literature we have needed a simple, brief, popular-level introduction—someone to provide us with an aerial view of the forest before we begin making our way among all the trees. This is what Jim Hamilton has done for us here. *What Is Biblical Theology?* provides a very helpful jump start for beginning students, and students of all levels will be blessed in the reminder of the marvelous patterns and themes that make Scripture such a glorious book."

Fred G. Zaspel, Pastor, Reformed Baptist Church, Franconia, Pennsylvania

"I am truly amazed at all that Jim Hamilton has packed into this little volume. *What Is Biblical Theology?* is an engagingly written distillation of years of both scholarly and devotional study of the Bible. The reader will find a succinct, clear, and compelling guide to the overarching story of Scripture. It will be at the top of my list of books to recommend for any who want to better understand the Bible, the world, and their place in God's story. This is a gift for which I am exceedingly thankful."

Rob Lister, Associate Professor of Biblical and Theological Studies, Talbot School of Theology

"Want to know your Bible better? Of course you do! Jim Hamilton can help. *What Is Biblical Theology?* is a manual for seeing how the many books of the Bible tell the one story about Jesus Christ: who he is and what he has done. Dr. Hamilton will help you love Jesus more by understanding your Bible better."

C. J. Mahaney, Senior Pastor, Sovereign Grace Church, Louisville, Kentucky

WHAT IS BIBLICAL THEOLOGY?

A GUIDE TO THE BIBLE'S STORY, SYMBOLISM, AND PATTERNS

JAMES M. HAMILTON JR.

WHEATON, ILLINOIS

Cover design: Brandon Hill

Cover image: Brandon Hill Photos

First printing 2014

Printed in the United States of America

Unless otherwise indicated, Scripture quotations are from the ESV® Bible (*The Holy Bible, English Standard Version*®), copyright © 2001 by Crossway. 2011 Text Edition. Used by permission. All rights reserved.

Scripture quotations marked AT are the author's translation.

Trade paperback ISBN: 978-1-4335-3771-4
PDF ISBN: 978-1-4335-3772-1
Mobipocket ISBN: 978-1-4335-3773-8
ePub ISBN: 978-1-4335-3774-5

Library of Congress Cataloging-in-Publication Data

Hamilton, James M., 1974–
   What is biblical theology? : a guide to the Bible's story, symbolism, and patterns / James M. Hamilton Jr.
      pages cm
   Includes bibliographical references and index.
   ISBN 978-1-4335-3771-4 (tp)
    1. Bible—Theology. 2. Bible—Introductions. I. Title.
BS543.H3355   2014
230'.041—23   2013022763

Crossway is a publishing ministry of Good News Publishers.

VP		24	23	22	21	20	19	18	17	16	15	14
15	14	13	12	11	10	9	8	7	6	5	4	3	2	1

For Evie Caroline
our little girl
May it be granted you to clothe yourself
with fine linen, bright and pure,
for the wedding feast of the Lamb.
(Rev. 19:7–8)

CONTENTS

1

A BETTER WORLD
BREAKS THROUGH

Sitting uneasily in his chair, straining for breath, he tilted his head toward his wife, nodded in the direction of my three sons, and said, "It's good for them to be here."

Looking at me he continued, gasping out the words, "We wanted to hide things like this. But it's good for these boys to see me dying. Death is real."

Later that night, his wife of more than fifty years became a widow.

Knowing that life was leaving his body, he saw right through our medicated, sanitized, hedonistic culture. He could ignore death no longer, and he was convinced others shouldn't either. There was no avoiding it, so he looked it in the face and affirmed the goodness of the true story of the world. His approaching death was like a strong wind blowing away a fog of falsehood. A better understanding of the world broke through, as it had been doing since he was born again.

What we think and how we live is largely determined by the larger story in which we interpret our lives. Does your story enable you to look death in the face? Does your story give you a hope that goes beyond the grave?

In the throes of death that night, my older brother in Christ was rejecting false stories of the world. He refused to live his last moments informed by stories that would have people pretend death isn't real or fear what lies beyond it.

He wouldn't have put it in these words, but he was affirming that it is good for children to see that the Bible's story is real. That's what he meant when he said that it was good for my boys (ages six, three, and one at the time) to be there as his body fought through its failing moments.

Will it take the nearness of your own death for you to reject false stories in favor of reality?

The world does have a true story. The Bible tells it. This book is about the Bible's big story, and it's about how we become people who live in that story. To do biblical theology is to think about the whole story of the Bible. We want to understand the organic development of the Bible's teaching so that we are interpreting particular parts of the story in light of the whole. As an acorn grows into an oak tree, Genesis 3:15 grows into the good news of Jesus Christ.

One of the primary aims of biblical theology is to understand and embrace the worldview of the biblical authors. In order to do this, we have to know the story they take for granted, the connections they see between the events in that story, and the ways they read later parts of the story by the light that emanates from its earlier parts.

The Bible has a narrative arc that begins at creation, rises over all that has been and will be, and lands at the end of all things. The prophetic and poetic parts of the Bible provide interpretive commentary on the story, and the apocalypses unveil the way things are and will be.

The Bible's big story, this overarching narrative, is also built out of smaller stories. At the same time, the stories told in the Old Testament work together to set up a mystery resolved in Christ. Have you noticed the clues and hints that build to the climactic revelation?

Let's think more about what biblical theology is, and then we'll turn to the Bible's big story, the symbols that summarize and interpret the story, and the church's place in it.

2

WHAT IS BIBLICAL THEOLOGY?

What is biblical theology? The phrase *biblical theology* is used here to refer to the interpretive perspective of the biblical authors.

What is an "interpretive perspective"? It's the framework of assumptions and presuppositions, associations and identifications, truths and symbols that are taken for granted as an author or speaker describes the world and the events that take place in it.

What do the biblical authors use this perspective to interpret? First, the biblical authors have interpreted earlier Scripture, or in the case of the very first author on record (Moses), accounts of God's words and deeds that were passed down to him.

Second, they interpreted world history from creation to consummation.

And third, they interpreted the events and statements that they describe. Moses didn't recount *everything* that Balaam said and did in the instances presented in Numbers 22–24. Moses selected what he wanted, arranged it with care, and presented the true story. The presentation of Balaam's oracles that Moses gives us in the book of Numbers is already an interpretation of them, and because I believe that Moses was inspired by the Holy Spirit, I hold that his interpretation makes his account of the Balaam oracles *more* true, not less. More true because the way Moses selected, arranged, and presented (i.e., interpreted) enables his audience to see more clearly how what Balaam said and did fits into the true story of the world Moses tells in the Pentateuch.

To summarize, by the phrase *biblical theology* I mean the interpretive perspective reflected in the way the biblical authors have presented their understanding of earlier Scripture, redemptive history, and the events they are describing, recounting, celebrating, or addressing in narratives, poems, proverbs, letters, and apocalypses.

The previous sentence mentions various kinds of literature. The Bible is a book, and the men who wrote the sixty-six books that make up the Bible were engaged authors. That means we have to think about literature as we think about interpreting the Bible. A short guide like this cannot exhaust these topics, but it can point to the path and offer some thoughts on how to stay on it. Our struggle is not against flesh and blood. The study of biblical theology is like a quest to become someone who can pull down strongholds with weapons mighty to God. For the quest to succeed we must learn to destroy arguments and lofty opinions raised against the knowledge of God, taking every thought captive to the obedience of Christ (2 Cor. 10:3–5). Welcome to this entry point on the path toward becoming a biblical theologian. With the Lord's help, the quest will take you into another world, the thought-world that *is* biblical theology.

Here at the outset, let me say what biblical theology is not—in my opinion, anyway. Some use the phrase *biblical theology* to mean something other than what I have hinted at above. Though we're using the same phrase, we are coming at the subject very differently. By *biblical theology* I do not mean "my theology is more biblical than yours." Nor do I refer to that stick some biblicists keep at hand for whopping the unsuspecting systematic theologian who happens along (I once heard a biblical scholar declare, "Systematic theology is bad; biblical theology is good").

After the Enlightenment, certain ways of thinking about the world fell out of fashion in the academy. Particularly, the Bible's. Heretics who styled themselves as courageous free thinkers chucked ideas that had prevailed among students of the Bible—biblical ideas about God's sovereignty, the inspiration of Scripture, and the coherence and unity of the Bible's message.

The story the Bible tells was rejected, and an alternative was put in its place. The evidence for this alternative narrative exists in the "scholarly" imagination. This alternative narrative has its own time line, its own authors, and its own account of what really went down: evolutionary development, competing ideologies, the documentary hypothesis, and so forth. On this reading, what the biblical texts say and the story the Bible tells is mere propaganda.

We have seen a world of responses to the influence of the (so-called) Enlightenment on biblical interpretation. One might say the responses have ranged from pole to pole.

At the South Pole the liberal response to the Enlightenment was to develop the academic discipline of biblical theology as a way to sift the wheat from the chaff. Liberal academics sought to discern which parts of the Bible's theology remained relevant and which parts no longer were. Someone doing biblical theology in this way today might employ the method to argue that the Bible endorses same-sex marriage and denounces the use of fossil fuel. If the text as a whole is not authoritative, it easily conforms to our agenda.

From the North Pole, the conservative response to the Enlightenment at many points sought to use biblical theology to reassert the unity of the Bible. In an effort to establish common ground and persuade skeptics, conservatives (at least for the sake of argument) conceded the chucked ideas. They were trying to prove the Bible's coherence to those who thought its unity had been shattered, so they resorted to methods and assumptions developed by and approved in the unbelieving guild. These methods and assumptions naturally placed limits on what the Bible could say.

There is of course a vast terrain between these two poles, plenty of room for a variety of "biblical theological" programs. You might have a scholar trained at the South Pole (in a liberal environment) who critiques the excesses of "Antarctica" (the left) from a biblical theological perspective. Conservatives get really excited about these types. Or you might have a scholar trained on the North Pole denying the existence of true north. These scholars find themselves the darlings of post-evangelical publishers.

The thing to note about these poles is that they're on the same planet. That is, the biblical theologians going about their work these ways, whether starting from North Pole or South, are all living in the same world, breathing the same air, sharing the same assumptions. But what if biblical theology is a bridge going somewhere else? What if it's a way to get out of one world into another?

This book is not trying to be a compass you can use to go north or south. It's trying to help you find treasure in the trash. The way of thinking modeled and taught by the Bible's authors was scrapped, but when we pull these ideas out of the garbage, we find them worth more than the million-dollar painting *Tres Personajes* that Elizabeth Gibson found in the trash on the street in New York City.

Our aim is to trace out the contours of the network of assumptions reflected in the writings of the biblical authors. If we can see what the biblical authors assumed about story, symbol, and church, we will glimpse the world as they saw it. To catch a glimpse of the world as they saw it is to see the real world.

I hasten to add that the Holy Spirit inspired the biblical authors. That gave them a level of certainty about their interpretive conclusions that we cannot have about ours because the Holy Spirit does not inspire us and guarantee our inerrancy. If he did, our books would be added to the canon of Scripture, which is not happening. Still, we're called to follow the apostles as they followed Christ (cf. 1 Cor. 11:1), and part of doing that means learning to interpret Scripture, redemptive history, and the events that happen to us the way the biblical authors did, even if absolute certainty eludes us.

What I'm suggesting is that the Bible teaches Christians how the Bible should be read. Studying biblical theology is the best way to learn from the Bible how to read the Bible as a Christian should. By the same token, studying the Bible is the best way to learn biblical theology.

How should a follower of Jesus read the Bible? The way Jesus did. Jesus of Nazareth did not write any of the books in the Bible, but he taught the writers of the New Testament how to interpret earlier Scripture, redemptive history, and the events they were narrating and addressing. On the human level, Jesus learned the interpretive perspective he taught to his disciples from Moses and the Prophets.

So I'm arguing that the biblical authors operated from a shared interpretive perspective. They inhabited the same thought-world, breathed its air, and shared its assumptions. The world they lived in wasn't Darwin's. In their world we might find things for which we have no analogy and of which we have no experience. There is no analogy for the God of the Bible. He stands alone. We will experience him only if he reveals himself. In the Bible he has done just that. How do we come to know him? From his revelation of himself, from learning to read the Bible from the Bible itself. To learn to read the Bible is to learn to understand this world from the perspective of the biblical authors, which is to learn a divinely inspired perspective.

Moses learned and developed the ability to see the world this way from the accounts of God's words and deeds that he received, from his contemplation of what God had done in his own life, and from the inspiration of the Spirit of God. The biblical authors who followed Moses in the Old Testament, whether historians, prophets, psalmists, or sages, learned the interpretive perspective that Moses modeled for them and had it confirmed by other Scripture available to them. Jesus then learned to read the Bible, history, and life from Moses and the Prophets, and he taught this perspective to his followers (Luke 24). What we find in the New Testament, then, is Christ-taught, Spirit-inspired biblical interpretation.

The biblical authors model a perspective for interpreting the Bible, history, and current events. Should we adopt that perspective today? Absolutely. Why? I'm convinced that the biblical authors were inspired by the Holy Spirit, that God guided them to the truth by his Spirit, and that, therefore, they got it right.

I am confident that the apostles got it right and that those who would follow Jesus (Christians!) should follow the apostles as they followed Jesus (cf. 1 Cor. 11:1). I am also confident that as we try to follow Jesus by following the apostles, we will make mistakes. The history of interpretation is full of mistakes. We see through a glass darkly (1 Cor. 13:12). But again, the fact that the Spirit is not ensuring the inerrancy of our conclusions does not mean we should adopt an *un-* or *a*-biblical perspective when reading the Bible, thinking about redemptive history, or trying to understand our own lives. It does mean that we should hold our conclusions with humility, fight that manxome foe, and allow the Bible to correct us.

At this point I hope you want more—more of the Bible, mainly, but also more information on how to understand and embrace the network of assumptions modeled by the biblical authors. As mentioned above, a short book like this is a little like standing by that path that leads to the bridge that leads to a different world. The Jabberwock and the frumious

Bandersnatch prowl the path, and you can take your chances starting from this point. I'm writing this book because I'm convinced that the world to which this path leads is worth any risk to reach.

There are more detailed descriptions of this path, even guided tours of it, but for those with an opportunity and an adventurous spirit, here's what this book has for you. The rest of it falls into three parts: the first sets out the Bible's big story, the second looks at the way the biblical authors use symbols to summarize and interpret that story, and the third considers the part the church plays in that story.

So the three parts of this book can be put into three words: *story*, *symbol*, and *church*. There's obviously more that could be said about biblical theology, but these are the three things about the path to the bridge into another world we'll focus on here: the overarching metanarrative that is the Bible's big story, the way the biblical authors use key symbols to summarize and interpret that story, and the place of the church in it.

If biblical theology is a way to get into another world, the world inhabited by the biblical authors, you have a right to understand my intentions. My hope is that you cross the bridge into their thought-world and never come back. I hope you will breathe the air of the Bible's world, recognize it as the real Narnia, and never want to leave.

If this happens, you will have come to inhabit the Bible's story. My prayer is that its symbols and patterns will shape the way you view the world, and that your understanding of the church's place in story and symbol will make you know the riches of God's inheritance in the saints (Eph. 1:18), the great power "he worked in Christ when he raised him from the dead" (1:20), and the glory he displays in the church and in Christ Jesus forever (Eph. 3:21).

In brief, I hope that you will adopt the perspective of the biblical authors and that you will read the world from the Bible's perspective, rather than reading the Bible from the world's.

Part 1

THE BIBLE'S
BIG STORY

3

THE NARRATIVE

What's a narrative made of? Narratives have a setting, characterization, and plot. Plots are built out of episodes and conflict, and if successful they communicate themes.

SETTING

The Bible is set in the world as we know it. Most of its story happens on the three bodies of land around the Mediterranean Sea, but the story is about the whole world. The Bible presents an interpretation of its own setting that gets at the meaning and purpose of this world God created.

Shakespeare showed his genius in a theater named the Globe. The place was aptly named, as Shakespeare held the mirror up to nature and depicted the world as it is. The real world where God shows his genius is the archetype of the theater where Shakespeare showed his. God built this stage to show his craft. The world is a theater for the display of God's glory.

God built the set (created the world) so there would be a place where he is known, served, worshiped, and present. Places where gods are known, served, worshiped, and present are called temples. God built the earth as his temple, and in it he put his image and likeness. The realm that God has created is a cosmic temple; the image God put in the temple to represent himself is mankind. Everything God made was good, but the characters in the drama rebelled against God and defiled his temple. In response to the sin of Adam, God subjected creation to bondage, offering hope, however, that there would be a restoration.

Don't miss the connections between the setting and the characters. God made and owns the setting. It's his. It's for him. It's about him.

The worldwide setting of the Bible's story is presented as God's cosmic temple. The tabernacle and later the temple God gave to Israel were small-scale versions of the cosmos, microcosms (Ps. 78:69). This understanding of the story's setting has implications for the story's characters: that the world is a cosmic temple means that it's a place in which God is known, served, present, and worshiped. The human characters in the temple are the real thing imitated by idolaters who build temples to false gods and then put wood or stone "images" of those gods in those temples. In the real story, the image of God in God's temple is a living, breathing, worshiping human being. Then there are the enemies: the serpent and his seed are trying to usurp God, but all they accomplish is the (temporary) defilement of God's temple.

As the setting of the story is related to the characters in the story, so also the setting is key to the plot. The plot begins with the making of the cosmic temple, which is defiled by sin. Once it is defiled, however, God makes statements that hint at restoration. Eventually God gives to the nation of Israel a small-scale version of the setting, a microcosm, when he gives them first the tabernacle and later the temple. The judgments visited on the microcosms (when tabernacle and temple are destroyed) point forward to the judgment that God will bring on the macrocosm (the world), and then God will bring about a new and better cosmic temple, a new heaven and earth. At this restoration God will make things better than they were at the beginning.

CHARACTERS

No offense, but you aren't the main character in the big story of the world. One of the best things that can happen to us is discovering our role in the real story of the world.

The triune God is the protagonist of this cosmic drama, with Satan as the (infinitely outmatched) antagonist, and there are other heavenly beings involved in the story. God and Satan are locked in conflict, each seeking the allegiance of humans made in God's image. Protagonist and antagonist are contending for dominion over the world God made. It doesn't take a genius to predict victory for the Creator, but it takes the power of the Spirit to side with him.

Humans are either seed of the woman or seed of the serpent. The Hebrew word rendered "seed" or "offspring" or (less felicitously) "descendants" in English can refer to *one* "seed" or to *a handful* of "seed." There are individual (Gal. 3:16; Rev. 12:5) and collective (Rom. 16:20; Rev. 12:17) manifestations of the seed of the woman and the seed of the serpent in the Bible. There are good guys and bad guys.

Those who call on the name of the Lord (Gen. 4:26; Rom. 10:13) are "born of God" and "God's seed abides" in them

(1 John 3:9). They have been made alive by the Holy Spirit (John 3:5–8; Eph. 2:5). They are the collective seed of the woman against whom that ancient dragon, who is the Devil and Satan, rages (Rev. 12:17). They trust the singular seed of the woman, who saved them by crushing the serpent's head (Gen. 3:15; John 12:31). The guys in the black hats, rebels who gather together against the Lord and his anointed (Ps. 2:1–3), are the seed of the serpent (John 8:44). The serpent's seed are not literal snakes but people who speak and act like the dragon (cf. Rom. 16:17–20; Rev. 13:11). Like their father the Devil, they dishonor those whom God has blessed, and for that God curses them (Gen. 3:14–15; 4:11; 9:25; 12:3).

God cursed the serpent and his seed: to the serpent he said, "Cursed are you" (Gen. 3:14), and then he spoke the same words to Cain after Cain killed Abel (Gen. 4:11). Then Canaan was cursed after Ham's sin against Noah (Gen. 9:25), and God told Abraham that he would curse those who dishonored him (Gen. 12:3). Those who kill like Cain, exalt themselves like Lamech (Gen. 4:23), scoff like Ham, and oppose God's purposes by fighting against Abraham and his offspring are, in the figurative words of Jesus, of their father the Devil (John 8:44). They are seed of the serpent, or in the words of John the Baptist, a "brood of vipers" (Matt. 3:7).

By contrast, a line of descent is carefully traced through the Old Testament that begins from Adam, continues through Noah to Abraham, Isaac, and Jacob, carries on through David right down to Jesus the Messiah. The Bible's genealogies carefully preserve this line of descent from Adam to Jesus. Jesus is the singular seed of the woman. Those who embrace God's promises and align themselves with God's purposes identify with the Promised One by faith. They are the collective seed of the woman.

When God made the setting, the cosmic temple, he gave dominion over it to the man and the woman (Gen. 1:28). When they sinned, Satan took control as "the prince of the power of the air," and with him are the "sons of disobedience," the "children of wrath" (Eph. 2:2–3). God has promised, however, that the son of David will rule (Ps. 110). He will receive dominion over God's restored cosmic temple (Rev. 11:15–19).

What part do you play in this drama? Have you embraced the role you were made to enact, or are you trying to be God? Are you with God, who will triumph, or with Satan, who looks good for the time being?

PLOT

In broadest terms, the Bible's plot can be summarized in four words: *creation*, *fall*, *redemption*, and *restoration*. This isn't Satan's story. He has introduced the plot conflict that will be resolved. He will be defeated. Don't side with him, don't aid and abet his causes, and don't envy those who side with him.

God created a cosmic temple. God's good creation was defiled by sin that resulted from the temptation of the serpent, who turns out to be the archenemy seeking to usurp God's throne.

God responded to Satan's pride with the humility of Jesus. God answered the rebellion of Satan with the obedience of Jesus. All the misery and rage of Satan is overwhelmed by the grace and love of Jesus, who for the joy set before him endured the cross (Heb. 12:2). That cross is the plot's great twist: the long awaited hero came, and he was not only rejected but killed.

31

Killed dead. Put in the tomb. Then hope rose from the dead. The death of Christ was not his defeat but his conquest. God judged sin, condemned it, and Christ died on the cross to pay the penalty for it. Through the judgment that fell on Jesus, God saves all who will trust in him. The demands of justice satisfied by the death of the Son, the Father shows mercy to those who repent and believe. Jesus died to give abundant life (John 10:10), to complete joy (John 15:11).

One of God's great accomplishments as the author of all is that he brought this to pass. God orchestrated the events that accomplished salvation. He sent the Redeemer, who was not welcomed but rejected, not hailed but killed, and thereby God ensured the plot's resolution.

One of the great accomplishments of the biblical authors is that they are able to tell this story with such skill that we never recoil from the Bible, shake our heads, and set the story aside as unbelievable. The authors tell the story so well that we not only believe that the Jews rejected and killed their own Messiah but also understand how the events came to pass. It rings true.

The plot will culminate in the return of Jesus to judge his enemies and save his people. The people Jesus saves will know, serve, and worship God, seeing his face in a new cosmic temple, a new heaven and new earth. The plot will be resolved. The characters will be transformed into the image of Christ. And the world, the setting, will be made new.

Isn't it a relief that the world's plot is not limited to the brief span of our lives? We make sense of our days in light of this overarching narrative. The big plot of the Bible, with its guarantee of resurrection and new creation, gives confidence even in the face of death. The Bible's big story opens the windows on stale, stuffy rooms of deadlines and due dates, deaths and disappointments, and fresh winds of the creation-to-new-creation breezes blow through.

Now that we've overviewed the plot, we circle back for another look at the great conflict that drives it and at some of its key episodes, and in these we see its main theme.

4

PLOT: CONFLICT, EPISODES, AND THEME

CONFLICT

The prince of the power of the air, that ancient serpent who is the Devil and Satan, has engaged in a cosmic campaign to unseat the Lord of the universe, to take from God the Father what rightfully belongs to him. Satan and his seed are at war with God and his children (Eph. 6:12; 1 John 3:9–15).

In the mystery of his wisdom, God chooses mostly weak and insignificant people as his own. He wants no humans boasting (1 Cor. 1:29), and he wants us relying on him, not ourselves (2 Cor. 1:9). When God sets out to make a great nation of one man's descendants, he starts with a man whose wife is barren. When he wants to choose a king, he picks a young boy whose own father didn't think he would be king, and so when the prophet comes to anoint one of his sons, Jesse doesn't summon David until Samuel has passed over David's older brothers (1 Sam. 16:10–11). When God wants to save the world, he sends his Son to become a baby, born to a peasant girl in questionable circumstances, and he sends him not to a great world capital but to a small town in Galilee. It's almost as though God repeatedly gives a head start to the opponent who will never outrun him.

Satan always *seems* to have the upper hand. The seed of the serpent are always impressive by worldly standards, and they don't shrink from draconian tactics: Cain kills Abel; wicked Israelites reject Moses; Saul persecutes David; the Jewish leadership crucifies Jesus; and the world has treated Christians the way it responded to Jesus.

But God raises the dead, and if something is impossible with man, all things are possible with God. So in the face of what appears to be the triumph of the wicked, all the weakness and folly of love and humility and joy and hope show the power and wisdom of the true and living God, against whom no foe can prevail.

This happens over and over again, as can be seen when we look at the plot's episodes.

PLOT EPISODES

A plot is made up of events or episodes. Here I want to draw attention to five episodes in the Bible's plot: the exile from Eden, the exodus from Egypt, the exile from the land, the death of Jesus on the cross, and the promise of his return in glory.

Exile from Eden. Adam and his wife were in that perfect place with that one prohibition. They transgressed it. They tried to cover themselves. They heard footsteps. They panicked. They hid. God had made this place. They were accountable to him. They broke his law. He had promised death for that. They grabbed fig leaves. There was nowhere to go. He called—and into words of judgment he folded hope.

Exodus from Egypt. God sent ten plagues. The firstborn died.

The lamb's blood marked lintel posts. Unleavened bread was eaten in haste.

As at the flood, waters closed over rebels. As Noah was saved through those waters, Israel passed through the Red Sea on dry ground.

Later biblical authors treat the events of the exodus as a paradigm of God's salvation. The details are worthy of note: Moses floated in an ark covered with tar and pitch on waters where others died (shades of Noah). God humbled the strong and proud Pharaoh by means of the ten plagues and the death of the firstborn. God identified the nation of Israel as his firstborn son. The death of the Passover lamb redeemed the firstborn of Israel. The people fled into the wilderness having plundered the Egyptians and were baptized in the cloud and in the sea (1 Cor. 10:2).

In the wilderness God sustained his people on manna from heaven and water from the rock, spiritual food and drink that nourished hope for the promised Redeemer (1 Cor. 10:3–4). God entered into a covenant with Israel at Mount Sinai and gave instructions for the building of the tabernacle, symbol of the universe. God then filled the microcosm—the small-scale version of the cosmos—with his glory, showing Israel his purpose for all things. Israel journeyed toward the Land of Promise, which was held by giants, whom the small army with inferior technology overthrew by means of weak and foolish battle strategies (march around the city for seven days and the walls will fall down).

Exile from the land. Once in the Promised Land, Israel did exactly what Moses prophesied they would do (Deut. 4:26–31). The nation of Israel was like a new Adam in a new Eden.

Like Adam they transgressed. Like Adam they were driven out. Like Adam they left with words of hope folded into prophetic denunciations. Idolatry and immorality caused them to hear the footsteps, the sound of Yahweh coming in the cool of the day, but this time the footsteps were from tramping boots of soldiers. The prophets told them that God's judgment would be like a new flood: storm clouds would gather, the heavens go dark, and the waters overflow. It wasn't literal water but an army (Isa. 8:7–8). The foreign army left the cities desolate, the land waste, and the temple ruins. Exile from the land was like de-creation. The temple, symbol of the world, torn down. Sun dark, moon blood, mountains melted.

When God called Adam and Eve to account for their sin, words of hope came in the judgment God spoke over the snake. When God called Israel to account for their sin, words of hope came in the judgment God spoke through the prophets. Announcing that God would drive Israel from the land, the prophets also declared that God would save Israel again as he had done at the exodus—a new exodus (Isa. 11:11–16); that God would raise up for them a new David (Hos. 3:5); that Israel would enter into a new covenant with Yahweh (Jer. 31:31; Hos. 2:14–20); that as the Spirit was given to Moses and the seventy elders, he would be poured out on all flesh—a new experience of the Spirit (Joel 2:28–32); that there would be a new conquest of the land (Hos. 2:15), which itself would become a new Eden (Isa. 51:3; Ezek. 36:35). From all this we see a key truth worthy of italics: *Israel's prophets used the paradigm of Israel's past to predict Israel's future.*

The cross. In his teaching before the cross, and when he opened their minds after it (Luke 24), Jesus taught his disciples to understand him through the paradigmatic events of the fall, the flood, the exodus, and the exile. In other words, the events of Israel's history function like schematics or templates, and they are used to communicate the meaning of who Jesus was and what he accomplished. This is why John the Baptist prepared the way for Jesus with the words of a "return from exile" text (see the Baptist's use of the words of Isa. 40:3 in John 1:23). This is why Matthew highlights the way Jesus recapitulates the history of Israel—born of a virgin, threatened in infancy by Herod as the infant Moses was threatened by Pharaoh, called out of Egypt, tempted in the wilderness, hailed as a Lamb, cursed to exile in his death, raised to bring restoration.

God saved his people through the judgment that fell on Jesus, fulfilling the way he saved them through judgment at the fall, the flood, the exodus, and the exile.

Jesus is the new Adam whose obedience overcomes Adam's sin (Rom. 5:12–21). God identified Israel as his son, and Jesus came as Israel's representative, the Son of God. Jesus redeemed his people from the curse of the law by becoming a curse (Gal. 3:13), making it possible for the Gentiles to receive the blessing of Abraham in him (Gal. 3:14). Jesus typologically fulfilled the substitutionary death of the Passover lamb—not one of his bones was broken (John 19:36; 1 Cor. 5:7)—when he died to initiate the new exodus. The authors of the New Testament speak of Christians as those who are liberated from bondage, made alive, moving toward the Land of Promise, exiles returning to their true home, the city that has foundations. The whole story of the Bible hinges on the death and resurrection of Jesus to accomplish redemption, and it will culminate in the return of Jesus in judgment to consummate his kingdom.

The promised return. Daniel 7:13 speaks of a son of man coming on clouds of heaven to receive everlasting dominion (cf. Gen. 1:28), and in Acts 1:9–11, Jesus ascended to heaven and was received into the clouds, with an angel announcing that Jesus will come again as he was seen to go—on the clouds of heaven. The slain Lamb will come as the ruling Lion (Rev. 5:5–6). The humble servant will be King of kings. The last will be first, the least greatest. Enemies will be slain by the sword that comes from his mouth, rebels cast into the lake of fire. The worm won't die. The flames won't be quenched. *Hallelujahs* and *hosannas* ring, bells peal, trumpets blare, kingdom comes. Christ is Lord. He will reign.

THEME

What do these plot episodes have in common? In each God shows his glory by saving his people through judgment.

The severity and kindness of God shine in each of these episodes: God judged Adam and Eve by banishing them from the realm of life, Eden. Adam would return to the dust from which he was made, but he went out with a promise that the seed of the woman would crush the head of the serpent. This promise came in the word of judgment spoken to the serpent. The word of salvation, kindness, came in the word of judgment, severity.

And so it was at the exodus: Israel was redeemed through the death of the Passover lamb and the Egyptian firstborn. So also at the exile: as Adam left the garden with the promise, Israel was exiled from the land with prophecies of a glorious end-time restoration ringing in her ears. These instances of salvation through judgment pointed forward to the cross, where Jesus was judged so his people could be saved. When he returns, the salvation of his people will come through the judgment of the serpent and his seed.

The Bible is, of course, brimming with themes, and every one of them shimmers with God's glory. These themes all flow out of and feed back into the glory of God. Founding and launching them is the bedrock of God's justice, on which he builds a tower of mercy to make a name for himself. If there were no justice, if God did not keep his word and punish transgressors, there would be no such thing as mercy, for no one would need it since no one would stand condemned. If God were not just, he would not be holy, he would not be true or faithful, and there would be no such thing as a promise kept or a sinner justified by faith.

As God brings salvation through judgment, justice serves as the dark cloth on which God will display the diamond of mercy. The sparkling stone, the contrasting cloth, and the light that shines on both result in a breathtaking display of God's glory. The Bible's central theme is the glory of God in salvation through judgment.

God is going to fill the earth with the knowledge of his glory as he saves and judges. The world was created for this purpose, as the previews in the tabernacle and temple show. God himself announced that he would fill the earth with his glory (Num. 14:21). The seraphim proclaimed the earth full of his glory (Isa. 6:3). David looked to the day when his seed would reign and the earth be filled with the glory of Yahweh (Ps. 72:18–19). Isaiah said it would come to pass (Isa. 11:9), and Habakkuk echoed him (Hab. 2:14). God's ways are unsearchable, past finding out, and he owes nothing to anyone. He cannot be made a debtor or in any way bribed. From him, through him, and to him are all things. His is the glory forever (Rom. 11:33–36).

5

THE MYSTERY

WHAT ARE THESE GOLD COINS ON THE PATH?

As we read through the Bible, we find gold coin after gold coin on the pathway of biblical promises. These gold coins appear to have been minted in the same place, and as we examine them, we notice two things. First, there is a definite relationship between them. The later ones assume the design and impress of the earlier. Second, as we make our way through the development of the designs on the coins, we find that there are curious combinations of earliest and latest designs as well as a kind of story that can be traced through the images.

I am not talking about literal gold coins. I'm talking about the promises God makes about a coming Redeemer who will set things right and the way the growing pile of promises influenced later biblical authors as they chose what to include in their narratives. The earliest promises caused later biblical authors to notice patterns and similarities between earlier characters, with the result that the later authors highlighted similar patterns and characteristics in their own material.

When we see a later author present a repetition of an earlier pattern, which was informed by a promise, as readers we begin to sense that we are dealing with a sequence of events (a type, pattern, or schema) that the biblical authors saw to be significant, even if they were puzzled by it (cf. 1 Pet. 1:10–12). The repetition of these patterns creates a kind of template that represents the *type* of thing God does or the *type* of thing that happens to God's people. When we start thinking about what *typically* happens, we are dealing with *typology*, and since this is what has *typically* happened in the past, we begin to expect that this is the *type* of thing God will do in the future. That is, the type is prospective, forward looking, as it points beyond itself to its fulfillment.

The promises appear to have prompted the prophets to notice the patterns, so we might think of this as *promise-shaped typology*. Hearing the promises formed an expectation in the minds of the prophets, and then a pattern of events was interpreted in light of the expectation generated by the promises.

If this seems hazy, at points it is! The disciples of Jesus were surprised by what he did, and yet everything he did was foreshadowed in the Old Testament. We can't look at every gold coin in this short study, but let's examine a few.

MINTED BY ONE MAKER

Our aim here is to see the connections between key promises in the Old Testament that prompted prophets to recognize patterns. If a promise is a gold coin, then the presence of these promises in the Bible means that the biblical authors saw them as coming from God and relating to God's plan. This makes the promises like gold coins minted at the same place.

The earliest prophetic impress comes in the word of judgment God spoke to the snake in Genesis 3:15. The man and woman had every right to expect that they would die that day they ate of the fruit of the knowledge of good and evil (Gen. 2:17). But as God cursed the snake, Adam and his wife heard that there would be ongoing enmity between the snake and the woman, and between his seed and hers. Moreover, while the seed of the woman would be bruised on the heel, the serpent would receive a much more serious bruise on the head (Gen. 3:15). The ongoing enmity and the reference to the woman's seed both indicate that Adam and his wife would not die immediately but continue to live, though they had experienced spiritual death (Gen. 3:7–8). When Adam named his wife Eve, because she would be the mother of all the living (Gen. 3:20), he responded in faith to the word of judgment God spoke over the snake. Apparently faith came at the hearing of the word of the seed of the woman (Gen. 3:15; cf. Rom. 10:17). Adam and Eve believed they would not immediately experience physical death: they would live in conflict with the serpent, and their offspring would bruise his head.

Eve's responses to the birth of Cain (Gen. 4:1) and Seth (4:25) indicate that she was looking for her seed who would accomplish this victory over the tempter. The line of descent from the woman is carefully traced in Genesis 5, and in Genesis 5:29 Lamech expresses a hope that his son Noah will be the one to bring relief from the curse stated in Genesis 3:17–19. When we read Genesis 5:29 in light of Genesis 3:14–19, it seems that those who are calling on the name of the Lord (Gen. 4:26) are looking for the seed of the woman whose bruising of the serpent's head (Gen. 3:15) will reverse the curse on the land (Gen. 5:29; cf. 3:17–19).

Another genealogy in Genesis 11 continues to trace the descent of the seed of the woman. Then God's promises to Abraham in Genesis 12:1–3, like a pile of gold coins on the path, answer the curses of Genesis 3:14–19 point for point:

- Answering the enmity God put between the seed of the woman and the serpent and his seed (Gen. 3:15), God promises to bless those who bless Abraham and curse those who curse him (Gen. 12:3).
- Answering the difficulty God put in childbearing and marital relations (3:16), God promises to make Abraham into a great nation (12:2) and to bless all the families of the earth in him (12:3).
- Answering the curse on the land (3:17–19), God's promise that Abraham will be a great nation also implies territory (12:2), and a few verses later (12:7) God promises to give the land to Abraham and his seed.

After Abraham's death, God promised to confirm to Isaac the oath he made to Abraham (Gen. 26:3–4), and then Isaac passed the blessing of Abraham on to his son Jacob (28:3–4).

With these coins in hand, we can set them side by side and see that in addition to being promises of God, they set a story in motion. The promises apparently caused Moses to recognize a pattern.

Moses appears to have heard that there would be enmity between the seed of the serpent and the seed of the woman. So he noticed—and for that reason recorded—the way the seed of the serpent persecuted the seed of the woman: Cain killed Abel; Ham mocked Noah, as Ishmael did Isaac; Esau wanted to kill Jacob. This pattern of persecution probably prompted Moses to notice the way Joseph's brothers responded to him, prodding Moses to give extended treatment to the suffering and exaltation of Joseph. His brothers wanted to kill him, but sold him into slavery instead. In Egypt, Joseph was exalted, blessed the whole world by providing food in the famine (cf. Gen. 12:3), and then forgave his brothers, preserving their lives from the curse on the land.

The blessing of Abraham had been passed to Isaac, then to Jacob, and Jacob appears to have bestowed it on the sons of Joseph (Gen. 48:15–16). God told Abraham that kings would come from him and Sarah (Gen. 17:6, 16), and we might expect the king to come from the line that receives the blessing. Surprisingly, however, when Jacob blessed his sons, he spoke of Judah in royal terms (Gen. 49:8–12). This prompts the explanation in 1 Chronicles 5:2 that though the birthright and blessing went to Joseph, the "chief" came from Judah.

In Numbers Moses gathers several gold coins and puts them side by side for us. As Balaam failed to curse Israel and blessed them instead, Moses presents him saying something in Numbers 24:9 that combines statements from the blessing of Judah in Genesis 49:9 with statements from the blessing of Abraham in Genesis 12:3. This means that Moses thought God was going to fulfill the promises to Abraham through the promised royal figure from Judah. Just a few verses later, in Numbers 24:17, head-crushing imagery from Genesis 3:15 is combined with language and imagery from the blessing of Judah in Genesis 49:8–12. Numbers 24:19 then speaks of the "dominion" this one from Jacob would exercise, showing that he would exercise the dominion God gave to Adam in Genesis 1:28. God would fulfill the promises to Abraham through the King from Judah, who is the seed of the woman who would crush the head of the serpent and his seed, and in this way

God would accomplish the purposes he began to pursue at creation.

A king from the line of Judah arose in Israel. On the way to becoming king, this young man, untested in battle, went out to meet the mighty Goliath, whose head he crushed with a stone, then removed with a sword. Like the seed of the woman who preceded him, David was then persecuted by the seed of the serpent (Saul), who chased him through the wilderness of Israel.

We are not the first to attempt to read these promises in light of the patterns. The biblical authors of the Psalms and the Prophets have blazed this trail for us.

THE PSALMISTS AND PROPHETS INTERPRETED THESE COINS

God made astonishing promises to David (2 Samuel 7). The prophets and psalmists interpret the promises to David and the patterns that preceded him to point forward to what God will accomplish when he brings these things to pass.

Psalm 72 seems to be David's prayer for Solomon (cf. the superscription and Ps. 72:20). David prays that the enemies of his son, the seed of promise (2 Samuel 7), will lick the dust like their father the Devil (Ps. 72:9; cf. Gen. 3:14). He prays that the oppressors will be crushed (Ps. 72:4; cf. Gen. 3:15). He prays that the seed of David will have a great name like what God promised to Abraham and that, as God promised to Abraham, the nations will be blessed in him (Ps. 72:17; cf. Gen. 12:1–3). All this culminates in David's prayer that God will accomplish what he set out to do at creation and fill the earth with his glory (Ps. 72:19; cf. Num. 14:21).

One example of prophetic interpretation of these passages, and there are many, is Isaiah 11. Isaiah clearly has the promises to David from 2 Samuel 7 in view when he speaks of the "shoot from the stump of Jesse" (Isa. 11:1). The Spirit of Yahweh will rest on him in fullness (11:2), and he will bring justice and peace (11:3–5). These events are likened later in the chapter to the exodus from Egypt (11:16), and they pertain to the regathering of Israel after the exile from the land (11:11). These realities make what Isaiah says in verse 8 all the more remarkable:

> The nursing child shall play over the hole of the cobra,
>> and the weaned child shall put his hand on the adder's
>> den.

When the King from Jesse arises to accomplish the new exodus and return from exile, it will be not merely a return from the exile from the land of Israel but also a return from the exile from Eden. When this King from David's line reigns, the enmity between the seed of the woman and the seed of the serpent introduced in Genesis 3:15 will be no more. That's what Isaiah is getting at when he speaks of babies playing with snakes and fearing no ill. Evil will be abolished. No more curse. And when God keeps the promise of Genesis 3:15 through the promises made to David in 2 Samuel 7, as in Psalm 72:19, so in Isaiah 11:9,

> the earth shall be full of the knowledge of the LORD
>> as the waters cover the sea.

Most of what I have said about promises to this point has to do with redemption. Similarly, most of what I have said about patterns to this point has to do with the persecution and suffering of those who cling to the promises, those through whom the promises will be fulfilled. The mystery is in the interweaving of these two lines of development.

DARK SAYINGS AND RIDDLES

So the promises are piling up to the conclusion that God is going to defeat evil and reopen the way to Eden when the seed of the woman arises to receive the blessing of Abraham, and this seed of the woman will come from the tribe of Judah and descend from David. How is this complicated, enigmatic, or difficult?

The mystery develops around two main questions: First, what is this business about the conqueror suffering? And second, how exactly are the Gentiles going to be blessed? The picture we seem to get from the Old Testament is one of the nation of Israel conquering all other nations, subjugating them to Yahweh and his good law by means of military might. The anointed One from David's line will rule them with an iron scepter (Ps. 2:8–9). The nations will come streaming to Zion to learn Yahweh's law (Isa. 2:1–4; cf. Deut. 4:6–8).

What's mysterious about this? For one thing, the program breaks down on Israel's disobedience. The nations can't see the glory of Yahweh's law because Israel has profaned Yahweh in their sight (cf. Ezek. 20:9). Rather than subject the nations to Israel, Yahweh subjects Israel to the nations and the nations drive Israel out of the land. Then when Israel does return to the land, their disobedience is seen as they intermarry with unrepentant idolaters from the nations (e.g., Ezra 9:11, 14). How are the nations going to be blessed in Abraham and in his seed (Gen. 22:17–18)?

The other aspect of the mystery is connected to this one. As noted above, the patterns were recognized in light of the prophecies. These patterns that were recognized had to do with the death of Abel and the persecution of Isaac, Jacob, Joseph, Moses, David, and others. It seems that David reflected on this pattern of suffering in the Psalms, especially those psalms that deal with "the righteous sufferer," such as Psalms 22 and 69 (there are many others).

Isaiah lived after David, and it appears that David's reflection on these things influenced the way that Isaiah developed prophecy and pattern in his depiction of the suffering servant. The "shoot from the stump of Jesse" of Isaiah 11:1 seems to be the "young plant, . . . a root out of dry ground" of Isaiah 53:2. What is remarkable here, and elsewhere in Isaiah, is the way the One who will reign in the restoration is also said to be stricken, smitten, and afflicted (53:4), bearing griefs and carrying sorrows (53:4), wounded for transgression, crushed for iniquity, and chastised for the healing of his people (53:5). The righteous One made many to be accounted righteous by bearing their iniquities (53:11). Before Jesus came to fulfill these prophecies, the Old Testament prophets puzzled over the mysteries (1 Pet. 1:10–11). The way the disciples of Jesus reacted to his announcement that he was going to Jerusalem to be crucified shows that they did not have this aspect of the mystery figured out.

The lines of promise and pattern point to conquest and suffering. Building on Isaiah, the angel Gabriel informs Daniel that the Messiah will be cut off and have nothing (Dan. 9:26). Similarly, Zechariah speaks of Israel looking on the Lord, "him whom they have pierced," and mourning over him "as one weeps over a firstborn" (Zech. 12:10). Zechariah goes on to speak of the Lord calling for the sword to be awakened against his shepherd, the man who stands next to him—the shepherd will be struck and the sheep scattered (13:7). As Isaiah said, "It was the will of the LORD to crush him" (Isa. 53:10).

PROMISE, PATTERN, MYSTERY

Perhaps summarizing the mysteries and highlighting the enigmas they represent will help us to contemplate them.

First, it's clear that a Redeemer has been promised. This Redeemer will defeat the Evil One and those aligned with him, and that defeat will roll back the curses and result in a new experience of Edenic life. The land will be fertile; people won't need weapons because they won't need to defend themselves or want to attack others; the King will reign in justice, establishing peace; and Yahweh's glory will cover the earth as the waters cover the sea.

Second, there is, however, the problem of the disobedience of the people of Israel in particular, and the sin of humanity in general. This problem results in man's exile from Eden, then Israel's exile from the land. If God is going to be true and just, these sins must be punished. Will exile from the land really pay God's people back double for all their sins, as Isaiah 40:1 indicates? Is there a way for God to punish sin *and* show mercy?

Third, what about this theme of the persecution and suffering of the seed of the woman? Abel died at Cain's hand. Joseph was lifted out of the pit and given to Gentiles. Moses was almost stoned by Israel. David was opposed first by Saul, then by Absalom. And then when God made promises to David, he mentioned something about discipline with the stripes of men (2 Sam. 7:14 ; the Hebrew term for "stripes" is used in Isa. 53:4, 8).

Fourth, in addition to the strong statements about how the Messiah will reign, along the lines of what we find in Psalms 2 and 110, we also have this mysterious talk about a suffering servant in Isaiah 53, a Messiah who will be cut off in Daniel 9:26, the Lord himself being pierced in Zechariah 12:10, and the sword awakened against the man who stands next to him in Zechariah 13:7, which speaks of a stricken shepherd and scattered sheep.

Fifth, what about the Gentiles? God said all the families of the earth would be blessed in the seed of Abraham (Gen. 12:3; 22:17–18), Isaiah says foreigners will be priests and Levites (Isa. 66:21), but at the end of the Old Testament Ezra and Nehemiah are making sure that Israelites don't intermarry with non-Israelites. How is God going to bless the Gentiles in Abraham's seed?

When we come to the end of the Old Testament, we have no answer to the question of how all these things will be resolved. How will the theme of the conquering Messiah be fulfilled in light of the pattern of suffering and the prophecies that the Messiah will even die? What about this new exodus and the promised return from exile?

WILL IT ALL FALL APART?

Has the story spun out of control? Or is there a way for the indications gleaned from these gold coins to be brought together into satisfying resolution?

The resolution is brought about by means of the greatest plot twist in the history of the universe: the conquest of the

Messiah that looked like defeat. Satan seemed to have conquered. He seemed to have bruised a lot more than the heel of the seed of the woman.

The way the disciples reacted to Jesus announcing that he would go to Jerusalem and die shows how unexpected God's secret stratagem was. Peter rebuked Jesus and told him it would never happen. It did.

Jesus fulfilled the pattern of the suffering seed of the woman. When he died on the cross he fulfilled the predictions that the Messiah would be cut off, the servant would suffer, the sword would awake against the man standing next to the Lord; indeed, those who saw him die looked on the Lord whom they had pierced. The sins of Israel were doubly paid (Isa. 40:2) because the death of Jesus provides complete forgiveness (Heb. 10:1–18). He died as the suffering servant (Isaiah 53). God called Israel his firstborn son (Ex. 4:23), and Jesus represented Israel as God's Son. The death of Jesus satisfies the wrath of God, finishing the curse against covenant-breaking Israel.

At the transfiguration, Moses and Elijah were discussing with Jesus the "*exodus* he was about to accomplish at Jerusalem" (Luke 9:31, AT). Jesus died as the Lamb of God in a new exodus that typologically fulfilled the exodus from Egypt. Jesus fulfilled the promises from the Old Testament that God would redeem his people in a way that would eclipse the exodus from Egypt (e.g., Jer. 16:14–15; 23:7–8).

The death of Jesus set the new exodus in motion, and the followers of Jesus are described in the New Testament as "exiles" (1 Pet. 1:1) who are being built into a new temple (1 Pet. 2:4–5) as they make their way toward the Land of Promise (1 Pet. 2:11), the new heavens and new earth, where righteousness dwells

(2 Pet. 3:13). When the authors of the New Testament speak this way, they are using the sequence of events that took place at the exodus from Egypt as an interpretive template to describe the significance of the salvation God has accomplished in Jesus.

And what about Gentiles? Well, Paul took the gospel first to the Jew, then the Greek (Rom. 1:16). When the Jews rejected the gospel, Paul went to the Gentiles (e.g., Acts 13:46). Paul teaches that when the full number of Gentiles have come in, Jesus will return and save his people (Rom. 11:25–27). All the families of the earth will be blessed in the seed of Abraham, Jesus the Messiah (Gal. 3:14–16).

Paul teaches in Ephesians that this was God's hidden plan for the Gentiles: the mystery has been unfolded to Paul and the other apostles and prophets (Eph. 3:4–6). Though it was hidden for ages and generations, believers now know the whole story (Col. 1:26). Knowing Christ means understanding God's great mystery (Col. 2:2–3). Moses prophesied it and displayed it in patterns, which were repeated in the histories and proclaimed in the prophets. Jesus fulfilled it all, and Paul explains that the mystery of God's will was this plan set forth in Christ for the fullness of time, so that all things (Jews and Gentiles), in heaven and on earth, would be united in Christ (Eph. 1:9–10). Gentile Christians enjoy all the blessings given to Israel in the Old Testament (Eph. 1:3–14).

When the gospel has been preached to all nations (Matt. 24:14), when the two witnesses have completed their testimony (Rev. 11:7), when all the martyrs have been faithful unto death (Rev. 6:11), when the full number of the Gentiles have come in (Rom. 11:25), Jesus will come. Living Jews will see him and believe, have their sins forgiven, and be brought into the new covenant: "and in this way all Israel will be saved" (Rom. 11:26–27). The trump shall resound, the Lord shall descend, the kingdom of this world will become the kingdom of our Lord and of his Christ, and he shall reign forever (Rev. 11:15).

NOT EVEN DEATH UNDOES IT

What God has accomplished in Jesus has brought resolution to the mystery left unresolved at the end of the Old Testament, and the consummation promised by the guarantee of the Holy Spirit will make all things new. The mystery has been solved, the outcome of the story has been revealed, and now we live in faith that the events that have been set in motion will bring to pass all our hopes (Rom. 8:18–30). We can live on these hopes because there is nothing that can turn God's love into disregard, not even death (Rom. 8:31–39).

Do you fear death? Do you think about your death, or the death of someone you love, in light of the Bible's big story?

Earlier in this book I related some of what happened the night of January 6, 2010, the night a friend of mine shuffled off his mortal coil. A few days later I had the privilege of preaching at his funeral. On that day we gathered to glorify God for giving us the joy of having known him.

Psalm 90:10 says,

The years of our life are seventy,
    or even by reason of strength eighty;
yet their span is but toil and trouble;
    they are soon gone, and we fly away.

By strength my friend lived to be eighty-one years old. He was faithful unto death. He trusted in Jesus Christ and faithfully served Kenwood Baptist Church as a deacon. He now serves in the presence of the King of kings and Lord of lords. He has taken his place in the heavenly court and sees the throne of the Majesty on high.

My friend's great conquest in life was overcoming the world. He rejected the world's lies in favor of God's truth. By trusting in Jesus, he conquered. His struggle is over. His battle is won. It was a lifelong epic conflict between good and evil, far more significant than any football game or election. At stake in his human life, as in every life, was the very glory of God.

He glorified God in his marriage. He loved his wife as Christ loved the church, giving himself up for her and being faithful to her to the end.

He glorified God in his commitment to Christ's church. He was always ready to do what he could to make disciples of Jesus.

He and his wife glorified God together by adopting a daughter, just as their heavenly father adopted them.

His body was active for eighty-one years, and now it's a corpse. We planted his lifeless remains in the ground, and the next thing those remains will experience is resurrection when Jesus returns, as described by the apostle Paul in 1 Corinthians 15:42–49.

Our first father was exiled from Eden. Israel was driven from the land. Every one of us lives outside the immediate presence of God. The Bible's story is our story, and the mystery has been made known.

The hero came, experienced the deepest, darkest moment of exile for us, forsaken by his Father, and then he inaugurated the return from exile by his resurrection from the dead. The

Lamb of God who takes away the sin of the world fulfilled the Passover, and we who believe have been liberated from slavery to sin. We are now traveling toward the Land of Promise. In order to understand how God leads us through this wilderness, we'll take up some of the Bible's symbols in part 2.

Part 2

THE BIBLE'S SYMBOLIC UNIVERSE

6

WHAT DO SYMBOLS DO?

Have you read *A Separate Peace*, by John Knowles?

Two friends, Gene and Phineas (nicknamed Finny), are in a tree. Gene shakes a branch, Finny falls and breaks his leg, and the halcyon innocence of the summer ends. Previously a great athlete, Finny will never play sports again. When he finally returns to school, the other students set up a mock trial to determine whether Gene caused Finny's fall. As it becomes evident that he did, Finny leaves in a huff, falls down a set of marble stairs, and breaks his leg again. Finny dies during the operation to set his leg. Finny's death gives Gene a certain peace.

I mention this book because it is so full of symbolism. A period of innocence ends with a fall at a significant tree. This is just like the garden of Eden. Then the death of the one sinned against gives peace to the one who caused the fall. I can remember my high school English teacher talking about how Finny was a Christ figure. Obviously the parallels aren't exact, but just as obviously, John Knowles knows how to use symbols.

As we turn our attention to symbolism, I am tempted to say that part 2 is also about figural interpretation, because it seems to me that the word *figural* has been used in the past to mean something very close to what I mean by the word *typological*. I hesitate to use the word *figural*, however, because while typological connections are usually established by direct appeals to textual evidence—exegetical features of the texts that forge the connections being interpreted—the word *figural* now seems to be used to refer to connections forged by the interpreter *apart from* exegetical details in the text.

I want to focus on what the biblical authors intended to communicate, on how they interpreted earlier Scripture and communicated its meaning through the symbols they employed. Symbolism is developed through the use of imagery and through the repetition of patterns and types, which will be looked at in the following chapters. Here we want to get our minds around what the use of symbolism accomplishes for the biblical authors.

Finny is called a "Christ figure" because of the way what happens to him corresponds to what happened to Jesus both in terms of the events that took place and in their significance for others. The tree is significant for the way it plays into the enmity between Gene and Finny: it's the scene of the crime, and the fall from the tree eventually leads to Finny's death.

If we don't understand a book's symbolism, we won't understand its author's message. This is true for *A Separate Peace*, and it's also true for the Bible. The Bible's symbolism summarizes and interprets the Bible's big story.

The Old Testament sets up a mystery, which is solved by what the New Testament reveals. God set forth a plan to unite all things in Christ in the fullness of time (Eph. 1:9–10). The Bible contains an overarching narrative. In the world God created, tension entered the narrative when Adam and Eve sinned and were driven out of God's presence in the garden of Eden. The grand resolution and climax of the story, the consummation of all things anticipated in the Prophets and described in Revelation, will be a return to God's presence in a new and better Eden.

Within this larger story, as a kind of variation on the theme, we have the story of God liberating Israel from Egypt at the exodus, then installing the nation of Israel as a new Adam in a kind of new Eden when the Israelites conquer the Promised Land. As Adam was exiled from Eden, Israel was exiled from the land. Israel's prophets announced that God would accomplish a new redemption like the exodus, and that this new exodus would result in returns from exile—return from the exile from the land of Israel *and* return from the exile from Eden.

At points the predictive descriptions of these two returns, to the land and to Eden, are presented side by side, as though they were to be one and the same. That turns out not to be the case. Israel returned to the land, but the exile awaited full remedy in Christ's death on the cross. The partial hardening of Israel, moreover, remains until the incoming of the full number of the Gentiles (Rom. 11:25; cf. Deut. 32:21; Isa. 6:9–11; Matt. 13:14–16; Acts 28:25–27). We are freed slaves, liberated by the new exodus, strangers and exiles on our way to the new and better Land of Promise, the new and better Eden, the new heaven and new earth.

As we attempt to follow the contours of the story the Bible tells, we must understand the symbols the biblical authors use as they tell the story. If we do not understand the symbols, we will fail to understand key parts of the story.

The symbols are used to summarize big ideas in pictures that the biblical authors intend their audiences to understand. In Leviticus, for instance, Moses does not explain the rationale behind the symbolic acts performed as the sacrifices were offered. He did not need to explain those actions, apparently because everyone in his audience understood the symbolism. We live in a different culture where blood sacrifice is not something we typically see. Thousands of years have passed. In order to understand Leviticus we must try to bring together everything Moses says about the sacrificial system to help us understand what is being symbolized (for more on this particular challenge, see my attempt in *God's Glory in Salvation through Judgment*, 107–14).

The symbols themselves tell a story, but what story do they tell? In this part of our consideration of biblical theology, we want to analyze the way the Bible's big story is reinforced and summarized by the symbolism the biblical authors build into the narrative. We will look at the images, types, and patterns the biblical authors employ to reinforce and summarize the Bible's big story.

The use of this symbolism produces what might be referred to as a "symbolic universe," that is, a set of symbols that explain and interpret the world by representing, or standing for, the world. To refer to the Bible's symbolic universe is to refer to the set of images, patterns, types, symbols, and signifiers that furnish the minds of the biblical authors. We want to understand this because we want to see the world the way they did, and we want to think about it that way, too. As we seek to understand and embrace the worldview reflected in the writings of the biblical authors, we are seeking to understand and embrace their symbolic universe.

In order to understand the Bible's symbolic universe, which summarizes and interprets the meaning of the world as it really is, we will look at the images, types, and patterns in the Bible. These images, types, and patterns are often laid on top of each other, and this layering both interprets and communicates. This use of symbolism and imagery adds texture to the story the Bible tells, reinforcing it and making it concrete.

A symbol, after all, is something used to stand in for a whole set of things. For instance, for some reason the symbol of one political party in the United States is a donkey, just as the symbol of the other is an elephant. When we see these symbols, any number of things might be called to mind: a particular politician, a set of beliefs and policies associated with a political party, or even a relative or friend who votes for that party. The point is that the little donkey stands for, or symbolizes, a lot more than some mule on a farm somewhere.

If we want to understand the Bible, we have to consider what its symbols stand for, what story they're telling, and how they're interpreting and summarizing what has gone before as they point to what is and will be. We'll begin with imagery before turning to typology, then patterns.

7

IMAGERY

Does this talk about symbolism seem abstract? Does the Bible's big story seem abstract? The images the Bible uses are meant to give real-world illustrations of these abstract concepts. So it's as though the biblical authors are recognizing that things are complicated, and they're trying to help their audience understand by using examples. Take a tree, for instance.

A TREE, A ROOT, AND A BRANCH

God's work in creation is related to his work in redemption. So at creation, we read: "God planted a garden in Eden . . . . And out of the ground the Lord God made to spring up every tree that is pleasant to the sight and good for food" (Gen. 2:8–9).

Then to help us understand that the nation of Israel, redeemed from Egypt, is like a new creation, Asaph talks about Israel as though the nation is a vine planted by the Lord:

> You brought a vine out of Egypt;
> you drove out the nations and planted it. (Ps. 80:8)

Isaiah also develops this image, presenting the Lord planting a vineyard in Isaiah 5:1–7. Because the vineyard produced rotten fruit (5:5), Isaiah is sent to harden the hearts of the people until they are driven into exile (6:9–12). This will be like the tree of Israel being chopped down and having its stump burned, but the holy seed is in that stump (6:13). The Lord is going to use the nation of Assyria as the axe that cuts down the tree of Israel (Isa. 10:5–15), but a shoot is going to come from the stump of Jesse, a branch that will bear fruit (Isa. 11:1–10). This shoot is both an individual and a symbol of a nation re-emerging. The king from David after exile stands for the reestablishment of the nation of Israel. Isaiah gets a lot of mileage out of branch imagery; as we have seen, he connects this shoot from the stump of Jesse to the suffering servant who bears the sin of the people in Isaiah 53 by likening the servant to "a root out of dry ground" (53:2).

This tree imagery is used all over the Bible. We've just seen how Isaiah talks about the Messiah as a shoot from the stump of Jesse. The judgment on the garden God planted in Isaiah 5, the tree chopped down in Isaiah 6, and the shoot from Jesse's stump in Isaiah 11 are all telling the story of Israel. The nation has broken the covenant God made with them at Sinai, so they will be exiled from the land. But God will keep the promises he made to David, when beyond exile a descendant of David will arise.

It may be that Isaiah was prompted to use tree imagery to describe the history and future of Israel and her Messiah because of the use of similar symbols in Psalms 1 and 2. These first two psalms introduce the whole book of Psalms. Psalm 2 is strongly messianic, and connections between Psalms 1 and 2, with the Davidic tinge of the whole Psalter, color Psalm 1 with a messianic hue. Psalm 1 describes the blessed man who meditates on the Torah as a tree planted by streams of water, yielding fruit in season and out. It's almost as though the blessed man who meditates on the Bible is a tree in God's garden.

This imagery interprets the story by connecting the cutting down of the nation of Israel (Isaiah 6, 10) to the holy seed in the stump that remains (Isa. 6:13). The imagery creates the impression that the fate of the nation stands or falls on the godliness of the king. It also reasserts the idea that the king stands for, or represents, the whole nation.

We Christians have good news: the shoot from the stump of Jesse is bearing fruit. The root out of dry ground bore our sins, and he perfectly fulfilled the Torah. His leaf will not wither and his fruit will not fail (cf. Isaiah 11, 53; Psalm 1). We can trust Jesus.

We Christians are also called to follow Jesus, the blessed man who meditated on the Bible day and night. We are to be flourishing trees like Jesus, and we get that way by giving our brains to the Bible.

The Bible says that those who are not Christians will be like chaff that the wind drives away (Ps. 1:4–5). We want to be trees planted by streams of living water, not chaff blown by the wind.

The tree God planted in the garden grows into a symbol of the redeemed nation of Israel and the One who would redeem both Israel and the nations, granting them access to the tree of life (Rev. 22:2).

There are also decisive acts of judgment that come to symbolize the visitation of God's wrath against rebels. Take the flood, for example.

THE FLOOD

Just as there is a connection between creation and redemption, there is a connection between judgment and de-creation. Moses communicates this by describing the flood so that his audience will see significant points of contact between the original creation and the new world that appears once the flood waters recede.

Consider these parallels between the creation and flood narratives: God parted the waters to make dry land appear in Genesis 1:9–10, and the Spirit was hovering over creation in 1:2; after the flood, God sent the wind/spirit to cause the waters to recede and the dry ground again appeared in Genesis 8:2–3. God had commanded Adam to be fruitful and multiply in Genesis 1:28, and he gives the same command to Noah in 9:1 and 9:7. As Adam sinned by eating of the tree in Genesis 3, Noah also sinned by abusing the fruit of the vine in Genesis 9. In both cases, nakedness was exposed then covered. God's judgment was visited in the waters of the flood, but the flood did not wash away human sin.

Moses wants his audience to see the correspondences between Adam and Noah. These correspondences hint that God's judgment is a kind of de-creation, while redemption is a kind of new creation.

Moses also wants his audience to see the correspondences between Noah and himself, so he uses the same term to describe both Noah's ark (Gen. 6:14) and the basket into which his mother put him (Ex. 2:3). Like Noah, who was saved through the waters in that ark, waters in which all Noah's contemporaries died, Moses was saved through the waters in an ark, waters in which the contemporaries of Moses died. Like Noah, who came out of the ark and entered into a covenant with God in Genesis 9, Moses came out of the ark and entered into a covenant with God in Exodus 20–24. Like Noah, who entered a new creation when he got off the ark, Moses led Israel to a shadow of the new creation as he took them to the Land of Promise. At the flood and at the exodus from Egypt, God saved his people through judgment.

Later biblical authors use the imagery of the flood to point to future visitations of God's judgment. As at the flood and the exodus, God will save his people through these subsequent judgments and enter into a new covenant with them.

We see flood imagery in the Prophets and the Psalms when foreign armies are described as a flood that will sweep through Israel (e.g., Psalm 124; Isaiah 8). These enemies are going to wash over Israel like a torrent of destroying waters because Israel has broken the covenant. Here again the imagery of the flood is used to summarize and interpret the Bible's narrative.

This reality is not limited to the Old Testament: Jesus spoke of his death as a baptism (e.g., Mark 10:38–39), which means that Jesus described his death as an immersion in the waters of God's judgment. Jesus died under the full weight of God's wrath against sin. The death of Jesus is the fulfillment of what Noah's flood anticipated. This is the judgment through which God saves his people. When believers are baptized by faith into Jesus, they are united to him in his experience of the flood-waters of God's wrath. This is why Peter says that the flood corresponds to baptism, which now saves us (1 Pet. 3:20–21).

The flood interprets and explains the Bible's story line: sin, judgment through which salvation comes, new covenant, new creation. The flood also anticipates the waters of God's wrath that will be visited on Israel through foreign armies, which waters of wrath will find their fulfillment in the baptism of Jesus as he dies on the cross. Just as Noah was saved through the visitation of God's wrath on the world, those who believe in Jesus are saved through the visitation of God's wrath at the cross. The flood also points forward to the culmination of the story. Peter explains that the "the world that then existed was deluged with water and perished" while "the heavens and earth that now exist are stored up for fire, being kept until the day of judgment and destruction of the ungodly" (2 Pet. 3:6–7). God purified the world by water at the flood, and he will purify it by fire in the future.

The tree and the flood are historical realities that come to be used in the imagery of the biblical authors as they connect creation to new creation while interpreting the story that spans from beginning to end. Both tree and flood summarize and interpret the story while forging connections between creation and redemption and judgment. The biblical authors also use tabernacle and temple to symbolize the world God made as the setting for this story of creation, fall, redemption, and restoration.

THE TEMPLE AND THE IMAGE WITHIN IT

The world is a cosmic temple. Reflecting assumptions common in the ancient Near East, and showing that he saw the literary connections Moses built into his narratives of Eden and the tabernacle in Genesis and Exodus, Asaph writes of the temple in Jerusalem,

> He built his sanctuary like the high heavens,
> like the earth, which he has founded forever. (Ps. 78:69)

This comparison reflects a profound theological reality: the temple is meant to be an image of the cosmos. The temple and, earlier, the tabernacle were small-scale versions of the world God made. Isaiah saw this same reality. The Lord's footstool is the ark of the covenant in the Most Holy Place in the temple (cf. 1 Chron. 28:2), but Isaiah knows that the earth was built to be God's dwelling place. The Lord says through Isaiah:

> Thus says the LORD:
> "Heaven is my throne,
>   and the earth is my footstool;
> what is the house that you would build for me,
>   and what is the place of my rest?" (Isa. 66:1)

The place of God's rest was the world that he built (Gen. 2:3). This idea that the world is God's global dwelling place is also what we see when the New Jerusalem comes down from God out of heaven, and the dimensions and adornments of the new heaven and earth show it to be a massive Most Holy Place. There is no temple there, but God and the Lamb are the temple (Rev. 21:9–27). This is why the bells of the horses in the New Jerusalem will bear the inscription put on the high priest's headgear (Zech. 14:20; cf. Ex. 28:36).

The idea that creation is a temple also helps us understand humanity, the image of God. Those who worship idols put carved and decorated pieces of wood or stone in their temples to represent their gods. In the world's true story, the living God puts his living image in the cosmic temple: a walking, talking, worshiping human being. God's image represents him in his temple.

Once again the symbol, in this case the temple, summarizes and exposits the Bible's story: when the glory of God filled the tabernacle and, later, the temple (Ex. 40:34; 1 Kings 8:10–11),

God gave Israel a preview of the way he will fill the cosmic temple with his glory. What God did in the microcosm, he will do in the macrocosm. What God portrayed in the symbol, he will fulfill in reality.

Israel broke the covenant, so God drove the people into exile. The culmination of the conquest of Jerusalem was the destruction of the temple (2 Kings 25:9). As the prophets point forward to the destruction of the temple, they talk as though the world will be torn down when God judges Israel for its sin. One passage that captures this is Jeremiah 4:23, which describes the world being returned to the Genesis 1:2 state of being "without form and void" when God visits his judgment. This is why there will be darkness (e.g., Amos 8:9) as there was before God made light, why the earth will quake and the stars be gone (Joel 2:10), as the mountains will melt (Mic. 1:3–4), and no one can stand (Nah. 1:6).

The Babylonians tore down the temple when they destroyed Jerusalem in 586 BC. Because the temple symbolizes the cosmos, the tearing down of the temple points forward to the tearing down of the world. This understanding of the symbolism enables us to understand the cosmic imagery the Old Testament prophets use to get at the meaning of the threats to the temple. When the temple was torn down, God's judgment fell in de-creating destruction. What happened to the symbol will happen to what the symbol represents when, as Peter says, "the heavens will be set on fire and dissolved, and the heavenly bodies will melt as they burn" (2 Pet. 3:12).

Between the destruction of the temple in 586 BC and the great day, however, we see another time when the sky went black, the earth shook, and this time the man who himself had symbolically replaced the temple was destroyed. Jesus spoke of his death as the destruction of the temple in John 2:19 because his death fulfilled the visitation of God's wrath against sin anticipated by the destruction of the temple in 586 BC. The death of Jesus saves all who trust in him from the final visitation of God's wrath on the great day, when God will burn down the cosmic temple.

SHADOWS AND SUBSTANCE

The tree, the flood, and the temple are shadows, but the substance belongs to Christ (Col. 2:17), the image of the invisible God (Col. 1:15).

Jesus is now building a new temple, not a building but believers. We are God's temple, and God's Spirit dwells in us (1 Cor. 3:16; 6:19). Think on the holiness of the Old Testament tabernacle and temple. Only priests can enter the holy place, only the high priest can enter the Most Holy Place, and only once a year. Is your life characterized by the holiness necessary for the dwelling place of God? Without that holiness no one will see the Lord (Heb. 12:14).

Be not discouraged. The old covenant dwelling of God was purified by the sacrifice offered on the Day of Atonement. The death of Christ has purified the new covenant temple. This is a blood that washes away every stain (Heb. 9–10). Trust it. Trust him.

Symbols summarize and interpret the Bible's big story. Key events in that story come to be used as images that connect creation to judgment and redemption. There are also key patterns that foreshadow the type of thing God's people come to understand him to do when he saves through judgment to show his glory.

8

TYPOLOGY

Everything described in these chapters on symbolism is related, at least loosely, to biblical typology. The flood is a type, as is the destruction of the temple. I have referred to these as "images" mainly because of their similarity to the tree imagery in the Bible. But even though the tree imagery is used to summarize and explain the Bible's story, a tree can hardly be considered a type.

The two key features of biblical typology are historical correspondence and escalation. The historical correspondence has to do with the way that real people, events, or institutions match one other—Noah and Moses really were preserved through waters in which others died, for instance. The escalation has to do with the way that as we move from the initial instance, which we might call the archetype, through the installments in the pattern that reinforce the significance of the archetype, we gather steam in the uphill climb until the type finds fulfillment in its ultimate expression. The import increases along the way from archetype to fulfillment.

FORESHADOWING FIGURES:
PEOPLE, EVENTS, AND INSTITUTIONS

The typology introduced in the Old Testament works like literary foreshadowing, but it is more than a mere literary device. Types are not arbitrary correspondences invented by the biblical authors but genuine accounts of what really took place. The biblical authors are drawing attention to people, events, and institutions where the divine author has caused actual resemblance. To examine biblical typology is to examine the orchestration of the sovereign God.

As people notice the *type* of thing God has done and interpret these patterns in light of the promises God has made, they begin to expect God to act in the future as he has acted in the past. This typological foreshadowing involves people, events, and institutions. Here we will consider examples of each.

People. Pharaoh tried to kill the baby Moses; Herod tried to kill the baby Jesus. Moses and his parents were strangers in the land of Egypt; Jesus and his parents were strangers in the land of Egypt. God summoned Moses to lead Israel, his firstborn son (Ex. 4:22), out of Egypt; God gave a dream to Mary's husband, Joseph, in response to which he led Jesus, God's beloved Son, out of Egypt (Matt. 2:15). Moses led the children of Israel through the waters of the Red Sea into the wilderness, where the people were tempted and sinned (Exodus 16–34); Jesus was baptized in the Jordan River by John, then went into the wilderness to be tempted by Satan, where he stood firm on God's Word (Matt. 3:13–4:11). At Mount Sinai, Moses went up on the mountain and came down with the Book of the Covenant (Exodus 19–24, esp. 24:7); Jesus "went up on the mountain, and when he sat down, his disciples came to him" (Matt. 5:1);

and Jesus taught his disciples the law of Christ (cf. 1 Cor. 9:21; Gal. 6:2) in the sermon on the mount (Matthew 5–7). These are some of the points of historical correspondence between Moses and Jesus.

There is also escalation from Moses to Jesus: Moses led Israel out of slavery in Egypt; Jesus saved his people from their slavery to sin. Moses led Israel into a shadow of the new Eden, the Land of Promise; Jesus will lead his people into the new and better Eden, the new heaven and earth.

Events. At the exodus from Egypt, after Moses was preserved from the attack on his life by the seed of the serpent, he was initially rejected by the people of Israel (Ex. 2:14). He went away, married a Gentile (Ex. 2:21), and then returned to lead Israel out of Egypt. The Lord struck down the firstborn of Egypt, passing over the firstborn of Israel because of the blood of the Passover lamb on the lintels of their houses. Israel was "baptized into Moses in the cloud and in the sea" (1 Cor. 10:2), and then the people ate "spiritual food" and drank "spiritual drink" (10:3) as manna came from heaven and water from the rock. At Sinai, Israel entered into a covenant with Yahweh (Exodus 20–24), and the nation received instructions for (Exodus 25–31) and then built (Exodus 35–40) the tabernacle.

What Jesus has accomplished is the typological fulfillment of the exodus because there is historical correspondence between the events and an escalation of their significance. Jesus was preserved from the attack on his life by the seed of the serpent, and the people of Israel initially rejected him. Paul teaches, however, that when Jesus returns, all Israel will be saved (Rom. 11:25–27). For the present, Jesus has a predominantly Gentile church for his bride. Paul identifies Jesus as our Passover Lamb (1 Cor. 5:7), and those who believe in Jesus have been baptized into him. We partake of a better spiritual food and drink in the Lord's Supper, and in the law of Christ we have received a better law that came with a better covenant (Hebrews 8–9, esp. 8:6). The church is being built into a new temple (e.g., 1 Cor. 3:16; 1 Pet. 2:4–5).

Here too the Old Testament archetype and its fulfillment in Christ in his death and resurrection are pointing forward to the consummation of all things, as the book of Revelation also presents God's final outpouring of wrath in an exodus pattern, with the judgments that accompany the trumpets and bowls corresponding to the plagues on Egypt. At the exodus from Egypt God saved his people from slavery to the Egyptians. At the new exodus Jesus accomplished on the cross (cf. Luke 9:31), God saved his people from their sins. At the exodus from the present age God will save his people from bondage to corruption (Rom. 8:18–25; Rev. 20:14–21:8).

Jesus is a new and better Moses who has offered a new and better sacrifice because he is the new and better priest mediating a new and better covenant as we progress toward the new and better land. Jesus is also a new and better David, and he is leading us into a new and better kingdom, one that will never be shaken.

Institutions. Both the priesthood and the sacrificial system given to Old Testament Israel are shadows pointing forward to better realities in Christ (cf. Heb. 10:1). In Hebrews 5–7 the author explains how Jesus fulfills the priesthood and replaces it, and in Hebrews 9–10 the writer elaborates on how the death of Christ on the cross is a better sacrifice, fulfilling the Levitical system and bringing it to an end:

- New and better Moses
- New and better David
- New and better Priest
- New and better sacrifice
- New and better law
- New and better covenant

NOT ONE OF HIS BONES SHALL BE BROKEN

We've looked at examples of people, events, and institutions that feed into biblical typology, but this should not lead us to conclude that these are three unrelated categories. Sometimes people, events, and institutions are interwoven, as in the case of the example we consider now. I hope to show that the event of the exodus, the instituted feast of Passover, and the person of David all feed into what John says about how the death of Jesus is the typological fulfillment of the exodus, the Passover, and David's suffering and deliverance.

The authors of the New Testament are constantly claiming that the Old Testament has been fulfilled. John 19:36 is a good example. The Roman soldier pierced Jesus's side (John 19:34). John insists that he saw it himself and is telling the truth (19:35), and then he writes, "For these things took place that the Scripture might be fulfilled: 'Not one of his bones will be broken.'" On reading that, most of us probably assume that the Old Testament predicted that none of the bones of the Messiah would be broken.

If we go look up the cross reference, however, we find that Exodus 12:46 is not predicting what will happen to the Messiah but giving instructions about the Passover lamb. What's going on here? The text John seems to claim as having been fulfilled is not even a prediction!

How is John interpreting Exodus 12:46? I submit that John is interpreting that verse the same way that David interpreted it in Psalm 34:20. Let me explain.

As I've mentioned, later biblical authors use the events of the exodus from Egypt as a paradigm for describing God's salvation. At several points we see this in the Psalms. We find a heavy use of exodus imagery in Psalm 18, from which I hope to establish this point, so that when we notice lighter use of exodus imagery in Psalm 34, we can posit that the same dynamic is at work.

In Psalm 18 David is describing how the Lord "rescued him from the hand of all his enemies, and from Saul" (Psalm 18 superscription). David begins by professing his love for the Lord (18:1–3), then uses metaphors to describe the difficulties he faced (18:4–5) and relates how he called upon Yahweh (18:6). As David describes the Lord answering his prayers in Psalm 18:7–15, he uses imagery from the account of the way Yahweh appeared to Israel at Mount Sinai in Exodus 19:16–20.

The trembling of the mountain (Ps. 18:7; cf. Ex. 19:18), the smoke (Ps. 18:8; cf. Ex. 19:18), the lightning and thunder and fire and the Lord coming down (Ps. 18:8–14; cf. Ex. 19:16–20)—all this imagery comes right out of the Sinai theophany. But it goes deeper than just a reuse of a description of God appearing on behalf of his people. Since Exodus 19–24 recounts how God made a covenant with Israel, David might be connecting the way God made a covenant with Israel and the way God made a covenant with him (2 Samuel 7; Ps. 89:3).

David goes on to describe the Lord delivering him, and he likens it to the parting of the Red Sea (Ps. 18:15; cf. Ex. 15:8), to his being drawn out of the waters as Moses was (Ps. 18:16; cf.

Ex. 2:10), and to the Lord taking him into a broad place like the Land of Promise (Ps. 18:19). What is David doing? He's describing the Lord delivering him from Saul and all his enemies (Psalm 18 superscription), and he's using the events of the exodus from Egypt, the covenant at Sinai, and the conquest of the land as a kind of interpretive schema to describe the way the Lord saved him.

David employs similar imagery, though less of it, in Psalm 34. In Psalm 34 he is describing another instance in which he was in danger and the Lord preserved him (Psalm 34 superscription). He blesses the Lord (34:1–3), then relates how he cried out to the Lord for help (34:4–6). David next makes a statement that summarizes how the Lord protected Israel from Egypt as they were trapped between Pharaoh's chariots and the Red Sea. Exodus 14:19–20 relates how

> the angel of God who was going before the host of Israel moved and went behind them, and the pillar of cloud moved from before them and stood behind them, coming between the host of Egypt and the host of Israel. And there was the cloud and the darkness. And it lit up the night without one coming near the other all night.

If we wanted to put this poetically, we would have a hard time improving on what David says in Psalm 34:7:

> The angel of the LORD encamps
>   around those who fear him, and delivers them.

Were it not for what David goes on to say in Psalm 34:20, we might think there was nothing more to this than a reuse of imagery. In verse 20, however, David uses the language and imagery of the instructions for the Passover lamb in Exodus 12:46 when he describes the Lord preserving the righteous:

> He keeps all his bones;
> not one of them is broken. (Ps. 34:20)

How do we get from the statements about the Passover lamb in Exodus 12:46 to the reuse of that language and imagery in Psalm 34:20? Let's consider the verses right before Psalm 34:20.

Psalm 34:18 speaks of the Lord being near "the brokenhearted" and saving "the crushed in spirit." In Hebrew these terms are in the plural, which means that David is referring to all those who side with him, those who take refuge in (Ps. 34:8) and fear the Lord (34:9) and turn from their sin (34:14). But then in Psalm 34:19 there is a switch from the plural to the singular:

> Many are the afflictions of the righteous,
> but the LORD delivers him out of them all.

This switch to the singular moves the focus from those who are suffering with David (Ps. 34:18; cf. 1 Sam. 22:1–2) to David himself (Ps. 34:19). David represents those who have aligned themselves with him. When David is delivered from his enemies, all those who side with David will be safe as well.

When David uses the Passover lamb imagery in Psalm 34:20, and as in verse 19 the terms are singular not plural, he seems to be speaking of his own preservation as though he is a kind of Passover lamb for those who are aligned with him. It is almost as though David is speaking of the Lord delivering him from his enemies as though it's a new exodus. Perhaps

David does not expect to die, but he is suffering at the hands of his enemies and knows that there is more coming before his deliverance. He confidently expects to be brought through the persecution and affliction, just as God saved Israel at the exodus from Egypt. When God delivers David, the wicked will be slain (Ps. 34:21) and the life of the servants of the Lord will be *redeemed*—and we know where God redeemed his servants: at the exodus (Ps. 34:22).

The point is that in Psalms 18 and 34 David describes how the Lord saved him, the events of the exodus serving as a kind of template or paradigm or schema. The salvation that God accomplished for Israel at the exodus is the archetype. David then interprets and describes his own deliverance in terms drawn from the archetype, making the deliverance the Lord accomplished for David an installment in the typological pattern of the exodus. As we have seen, the Prophets describe the future deliverance the Lord will accomplish for Israel after the exile as another installment in that typological pattern. And in John 19:36, John is claiming that Jesus has fulfilled this pattern in his death on the cross.

John is not claiming that Exodus 12:46 is a prediction that the bones of Jesus will not be broken. John is claiming that Jesus is the typological fulfillment, or antitype, of the Passover lamb. The death of Jesus fulfills the death of the lamb. The exodus from Egypt is the archetypal salvation God accomplishes for his people, and the death of Christ on the cross is the fulfillment of what the exodus typified.

9

PATTERNS

In the previous chapter I distinguished *images* from types because of the use of tree imagery, and a tree is not exactly a type. In this chapter I am distinguishing *patterns* from types because the two patterns I want to consider here are very broad. These patterns, however, like other images examined above, could just as well be described as typological. The repetition of the pattern creates the impression that this is what typically happens, which causes people to notice it and expect more of it. Here I want to consider the pattern of Israel's feasts and the pattern of the righteous sufferer.

ISRAEL'S FEASTS

Deuteronomy 16:16 states that thrice yearly all males in Israel were to appear before the Lord for the feasts of Passover, Pentecost, and Booths. These were not the only feasts, but because they were the three to be celebrated yearly, we will focus on them here. Passover celebrated God's deliverance of Israel from Egypt. Pentecost is referred to as the Feast of Harvest elsewhere (Ex. 23:16). And Booths celebrated the way God provided for

Israel as the people lived in booths or tabernacles throughout the time of their wilderness wandering on the way to the Promised Land.

The yearly celebration of these feasts would keep Israel looking back to the way God saved them at the exodus, brought them through the wilderness, and gave them a fruitful land. Constantly reminding themselves of these things through the celebration of the feasts would create a mental grid through which they would interpret their lives and according to which they would expect God to act for them in the future.

Anyone with eyes to see could tell that Israel needed to be delivered from more than just slavery in Egypt. There is a worse form of slavery—bondage to the worst of all taskmasters, sin. And anyone could see that while the Israelites were hoping that the curses would one day be rolled all the way back, that day had not yet come. The land had not yet bloomed, Eden-style.

The pattern of the yearly celebration of Passover, then, would symbolize and inform the hopes for a deeper redemption, and this is exactly what we find in Israel's prophets. The pattern of Booths would teach Israel that as God provided for them on their journey through the wilderness in the past, so he would provide for them on their journey through the wilderness after the new exodus. And so also with Pentecost, which pointed Israel forward to a day when the plowman would overtake the reaper (Amos 9:13).

Until that day, Israelites who studied the Scriptures would see a pattern of suffering in the lives of the righteous, and given the way that images, types, and patterns informed their symbolic understanding of the world, perhaps they would expect a fulfillment for this pattern too (cf. Simeon's expectation in Luke 2:34–35). That seems to be what we find in the Old Testament theme of the righteous sufferer.

THE RIGHTEOUS SUFFERER

Cain killed Abel. Abraham had trouble from the Philistines, and perhaps these were the days of the suffering of Job. Ishmael mocked Isaac. Esau wanted to kill Jacob, and Joseph's brothers sold him into slavery. The Israelites rejected Moses, as they did all the prophets who arose in his likeness: Elijah, Elisha, Isaiah, Jeremiah, and the rest. Well could Jesus say that Jerusalem was the city that stoned the prophets and killed those sent to her (Matt. 23:37), and he also prophesied that the blood of all the righteous, from the first martyr in the Old Testament, Abel, to the last, Zechariah, would be charged against the generation that put him to death (Luke 11:49–51).

This pattern of the righteous sufferer is particularly strong in the book of Psalms, where David speaks of his deliverance from persecution and affliction in terms reminiscent of the exodus from Egypt in Psalm 18:7–16 (cf. Psalm 18 superscription). And in Psalm 34 David uses imagery from the exodus (Ps. 34:7; cf. Ex. 14:19–20) and seems to depict his deliverance in terms that recall Israel being delivered by the Passover lamb (Ps. 34:20; cf. Ex. 12:46). As Jesus fulfilled the pattern of the righteous sufferer, dying as the Lamb of God to accomplish redemption in the new exodus, none of his bones were broken (John 19:34–36).

Jesus is the Savior to whom the feasts point: the Lamb of the new Passover at the new exodus, the bread from heaven and living water who tabernacled among us on our journey to the New Jerusalem, the first fruits of the resurrection from the dead. Jesus is the righteous sufferer. Being reviled he uttered no threats. And those who would follow him are to follow in his steps.

WHAT DO THE SYMBOLS TEACH US?

Symbolically speaking, then, the followers of Jesus are liberated slaves. The chains of sin have been broken. We have been bought with a price and are to glorify God with our bodies (1 Cor. 6:20). We are moving toward a new and better Eden, the new heaven and earth, and here we have no lasting city (cf. Heb. 13:14).

These symbols are given to us to shape our understanding of ourselves. They show us who we are. They give us our identity. They tell the story of our lives in the real world.

As we look toward a better city, we are called to follow in the footsteps of Jesus by suffering for doing what is good (1 Pet. 2:19–23). We are to take up our crosses and follow him (Mark 8:34), having in ourselves the same approach to obeying the Father and serving others that he modeled in obedience unto death (Phil. 2:1–11).

Biblical symbols are given to us to shape our understanding of how we are to live. Jesus is our paradigm, our pattern, our example. The symbols summarize and interpret the story, and they inform who we are in the story and how we are to enact our role in the outworking of its plot.

John Knowles's *A Separate Peace* opens with Gene returning to the tree out of which his friend Finny fell fifteen years earlier, leading to Finny's death. The book unfolds as Gene remembers the events surrounding that tree. But there's a bigger and better story, the archetypal one that gives rise to all the others: the great code. There's One who bore our sins in his body on a tree (1 Pet. 2:24) to save us from the fall that took place at the tree in the garden. There's a Savior whose death is more powerful than the one Finny died, and a forgiveness that gives not a separate peace but a whole and united one.

Part 3

THE BIBLE'S
LOVE STORY

10

A SONG FOR THE
LADY IN WAITING

The Bride of Christ and Biblical Theology

No one knows what happened to the mother. The baby girl was found in her blood. The kind father who found her—not her own father—literally gave her life. When the baby was found, the cord hadn't been cut or the birth blood washed from the newborn. The father provided everything necessary, and the child was adopted and raised in a safe and loving environment. The father who found her began to make plans to betroth her to his own son.

When she reached maturity, she took a tragic turn. She trusted her own beauty and sought to make a way for herself. Soon she was selling priceless things. Herself. Before long she was enslaved, hopeless, ruined.

Then the father who first found her bought her out of slavery. Having redeemed her, he did all he could to cleanse and purify her. And to her astonishment, he betrothed her to his son.

They were married and soon she conceived a child. Bringing him into the world was exhilarating and horrific. This was no ordinary child. Moreover, a dragon sought to devour him. Somehow the baby lived.

Imagine the world's great villain trying to kill her baby boy, and the boy living! After the boy escaped, the dragon turned on her. Somehow she lived too. Curses were overcome by blessings.

How had she eluded that dragon and made it to the wilderness? God only knows. Then once in the wilderness, all seemed lost as the flood rose, but then—God knows how—the earth opened its mouth and swallowed that flood. You might think her enemies were opposing God himself, their efforts always thwarted.

Do you recognize these events? Do they sound like Ezekiel 16 and Revelation 12? In Ezekiel 16 we find Israel personified as the baby girl found in her blood, to whom God gave life. Then when Israel grew to maturity, she committed spiritual adultery against the Lord. In Revelation 12, Mary symbolizes both Israel and the church. She gives birth to Jesus, and the dragon tries to eat him alive as soon as he is born. This bit about the dragon is a symbolic interpretation of Satan's efforts through Herod to kill Jesus. Then the mother, symbolizing the people of God, is preserved through the wilderness against all Satan's efforts to destroy her.

The Bible can be mystifying, can't it? The world and the events of our lives can be no less confusing. What are we to make of dragons trying to eat babies, of a woman carried on the wings of an eagle, of the wedding of a lamb? Do lambs get married?

Here's a leading question connected to the ones I've just asked: how are we to understand ourselves as the church? Now a slightly different, though related, question: if the church is so special in God's program, why does it seem so unimpressive?

If you're wondering what the main point of this section will be, let me come right out and say it: the Bible's story and symbolism teach us as the church to understand who we are, what we face, and how we should live as we wait for the coming of our King and Lord.

We looked at the Bible's story line in part 1, and at the way the Bible's symbolism—imagery, typology, and narrative patterns—summarizes and interprets that story line in part 2. Now in part 3 we explore how these things help us think about the church. We will do this on the basis of what we have seen of stories and symbols thus far.

As we think about the church in the story, these questions will help us reflect on the church's place in biblical theology: What part does the church play in the Bible's story? Who is she? What is her setting? What creates the tension in her part of the plot as the wider narrative develops? How is that tension resolved?

When we think about the way the biblical authors symbolize the church, we are exploring how the symbolism they used summarizes and interprets the church's place in the story. We don't merely want to think about story and symbol; we want to be swept up in them. We want to be identified by these symbols. Biblical theology is not just an interesting topic. It informs who we are and how we live. It's a way of getting out of a false world into the real one, a transporter enabling us to inhabit the story of the Scriptures. The Bible is the real *Hitch-*

hiker's Guide to the Galaxy, and biblical theology is the *Heart of Gold* that improbably moves us into the real world. We engage in biblical theology so as not to misinterpret what happens to us, seek our identity in the false world, and waste our lives.

The true story of the world and the church's place in it is a stupendous tale. Best of all, it's true. This true story of the world has more grief and joy, more drama and excitement, more hope and satisfaction than any other story the world has known.

The baby in her blood washed clean. The ruined lady renewed. The whore transformed into the pure bride because her betrothed died to save her. "This mystery is profound, and I am saying that it refers to Christ and the church" (Eph. 5:32).

Let's consider the church's identity, setting, and role in the plot.

11

THE CHURCH'S IDENTITY IN THE STORY

The church is a group of baptized believers in Jesus, right? Human beings. Those who believe, joined together in one hope in one Lord Jesus, sharing one faith, having experienced the same baptism, and worshiping one God by the power of one Spirit (cf. Eph. 4:4–6).

Following the Old Testament precedent of speaking of God's people metaphorically, Jesus and the apostles spoke of the church metaphorically. Metaphors identify things with what they are not. The point of a metaphor is to capture a truth about the thing metaphored. So God is not a stone, but the truth that God is stable, unchangeable, solid, and reliable is communicated when we say, "The LORD is my rock" (Ps. 18:2). Jesus and his apostles also used metaphors to communicate the truth about the church.

SHEEP OF THE SHEPHERD

For instance, Jesus might refer to his people as sheep, but they're not furry little animals on four legs; they're people.

Jesus calls his people sheep because sheep have characteristics that his people have. Sheep are cared for and led by shepherds, and Jesus is the Good Shepherd. Shepherds protect the sheep, even risking their own lives. Jesus laid down his life to protect his sheep.

Is Jesus your shepherd? Are you a Christian? If you're in doubt, I would encourage you to stop reading this book and go read Romans from beginning to end. Note especially the declaration in Romans 10:13 that "everyone who calls on the name of the Lord will be saved."

You won't find a better shepherd than Jesus. We want to be people formed by Psalm 23, confessing that the Lord is our shepherd, thinking of ourselves as those in his care, and living like it too.

BRIDE OF CHRIST

The church is a group of people, not an individual female making her way down the aisle. But the intimacy between Jesus and his people is approximated by marriage. Ephesians 5:22–33 teaches that the sacrificial love of Jesus for his people is to be reflected in a husband's love for his wife. The submission of the church to Jesus is to be reflected in a wife's submission to her husband. The wait between the identification of the people of Jesus and their final salvation is like the wait between the betrothal and the grand celebration of the wedding day (cf. Eph. 1:13–14).

For all these reasons and more, Jesus identifies himself as the Bridegroom when asked why his disciples don't fast (Mark 2:19), and he tells parables about a wedding feast to describe his coming kingdom (Matt. 22:1–14; 25:1–13). Paul says that the mystery of marriage is about Christ and the church (Eph. 5:22–33). Believers are depicted as pure virgins (Rev. 14:4), and when Jesus returns for his people, the multitude announces that the marriage of the Lamb has come and the bride has made herself ready (Rev. 19:7).

This metaphor of the church as a bride is meant to build our identity. We are to think of ourselves in bridal terms. We are not to commit spiritual adultery against the Lord Jesus. We are to save ourselves for the Bridegroom, as a bride saves herself for her husband.

BODY OF CHRIST

Paul's statement that marriage refers to Christ and the church (Eph. 5:32) immediately follows his quotation of Genesis 2:24, declaring that man and woman become one flesh in marriage (Eph. 5:31). This quotation of Genesis immediately follows the declaration, "We are members of his body" (Eph. 5:30), and earlier in the passage Paul refers to Christ as "the head of the church, his body" (5:23).

There is a connection, then, between the one-flesh union of a married man and woman and the union with Christ experienced by believers. The use of both the bride-and-bridegroom metaphor and the head-and-body metaphor in Ephesians 5 means that these are mutually interpretive. The head-and-body metaphor stresses Christ's leadership, to which the church submits (Eph. 5:24). The head directs the body, determining what the body will do, and the body puts in action what the head has decided (Col. 1:18).

The body metaphor also communicates the unity of the church (Col. 3:15). The church is one body that has been reconciled to God through the death of Christ (Eph. 2:16). There are not different bodies in the church, divided according to Jew and Gentile or black and white. The unity of the church transcends racial divisions (Eph. 3:6).

The ministry of the church is a process of the building up of the body (Eph. 4:12, 16). The various gifts of the Spirit given to the church are for this purpose (1 Cor. 12:1–31). The Spirit baptizes us into the body when we are united by faith to Christ in his death and resurrection as we are immersed in the baptismal waters (1 Cor. 12:12–13). The Father elects. The Son redeems. The Spirit seals.

Church membership is built on this body metaphor. Paul writes in 1 Corinthians 12:27, "Now you are the body of Christ and individually members of it." We are joined to one another and Christ. A Christian who is not a member of a church is like a hand or an eye that is not joined to the rest of the body. Can it live? Will it be useful?

We are united to one another by virtue of our union with Christ. We need one another the way a knee needs the rest of the leg, the way the leg needs the foot, and we must all be connected to the head, Christ.

These metaphors are to shape our understanding of ourselves. We are the bride of Christ, and we are his body, joined to him in a way that is approximated by the one-flesh union of a man and woman in marriage.

THE ADOPTED FAMILY OF GOD

The church is the bride and body of the Son, and its members are the adopted (Rom. 8:15), reborn children of the Father. This makes us part of the family of God (1 John 3:1, 10; 5:2), members of his household (Eph. 2:19).

This adoption formerly belonged to Israel (Rom. 9:4), whereby God identified Israel as his firstborn son (Ex. 4:22). In God's eternal plan, it is now the church that is adopted (Eph. 1:5).

We are not neglected. We are the sheep of the Good Shepherd.

We are not forsaken. We are the beloved of the Bridegroom.

We are not alone. We are members of his body.

We are not strangers. We are adopted into God's family.

If you're not a believer in Jesus, who looks after you? Who will come for you? To whom are you joined? Do you have a family? If you will repent of your sin and trust in Jesus, you can be part of the family of God.

TEMPLE OF THE HOLY SPIRIT

Jesus said, "I will build my church" (Matt. 16:18). He himself is its cornerstone, and the church is built on the foundation of the apostles and prophets (Eph. 2:20). The whole church is being joined together and growing to be a holy temple of the Lord (Eph. 2:21). The members of the church are living stones in this spiritual house, which is also a holy priesthood, offering spiritual sacrifices to God (1 Pet. 2:5).

We are not some barren, uninhabited, trackless waste. Our lives are inhabited by the living God. We are the temple of the Holy Spirit (1 Cor. 3:16). God inhabits our praises (Ps. 22:3).

As we believe the Bible, the Holy Spirit mediates the presence of Christ to us and fills us with God (Eph. 3:14–19). The idea that the church is the temple of the Holy Spirit is directly connected to the church's setting in the big story of the Bible.

12

THE CHURCH'S SETTING
IN THE STORY

The setting still concerns the whole world. When God put
Adam in the garden of Eden, Adam's responsibility was to expand its borders so that God's glory would cover the dry lands
as the waters cover the sea. Adam was cast out of the garden.
When God put Israel in the land, the nation's responsibility was
to expand its borders so that God's glory would cover the dry
lands as the waters cover the sea.

On the way to the land, God gave Israel a symbol of the
story's setting when he instructed the people to build the tabernacle as a representation of the world. The temple later replaced this tabernacle. God's presence in the tabernacle and the
temple required that everything in it be holy, and everything
around it clean.

The church is now the temple of the Holy Spirit, and
this speaks to God's presence in the church and the need
for holiness and discipline. Churches that do not discipline
jeopardize the lives of those who, like Nadab and Abihu
(Leviticus 10), disregard God's instructions as they approach

him and risk being consumed by an outburst of his holiness (cf. 1 Cor. 11:27–32).

These realities—that the temple is a symbol of the cosmos, and that the church is the temple of the Spirit—mean that the church is to be a preview of what the world is going to become. The church is a picture of the new temple. The redeemed who are in God's presence, who know him, enjoy him, serve him, and live for him—this is how the whole world will be in the coming age.

Just as God put Adam in the garden to extend its borders so that Yahweh's glory would cover the dry lands as the waters cover the sea, God put Israel in the land to take up that same task, giving them a preview of what it would look like when he filled tabernacle and temple with his glory. Jesus sent his disciples on the same errand to all nations: as disciples are made, the temple grows, the place of God's presence expands, and God's glory spreads over the dry land. In the age to come, these realities will be fully realized. The earth will be full of the knowledge of the glory of God.

The fact that the church is the temple of the Holy Spirit seems to inform what Paul says in 1 Corinthians 7:14 about unbelieving spouses being "sanctified." The unbeliever still needs to repent and believe (1 Cor. 7:16), but contagious holiness is imparted to the unbeliever by the believer with whom he or she is joined in marriage (7:14). These ideas also seem to be what Paul has in mind when he speaks of the children being "unclean" if they are not kept in contact with the temple of the Spirit, the believing parent.

We are no longer in a specific allotment of land, but our responsibility is still to cover the dry lands with God's glory as the waters cover the sea. The people of God are no longer a sociopolitical nation with boundaries. We are transnational. We are no longer an ethnic entity with a military. We are from all nations.

Under the old covenant, the nation of Israel subdued the nations round about by military conquest, bringing them under the authority of the law of the Lord. In the new covenant, the church has no military agenda. Rather, we seek to bring people to our point of view by persuading them to believe what we believe, convincing them to submit themselves to the Lord's authority.

We no longer go to the temple in Jerusalem to worship the Lord. Now we worship the Lord in Spirit and in truth wherever God's people gather (John 4:21–24).

Thinking about the setting also returns us to another aspect of our identity. We are no longer in bondage, but we are not yet home. We are like the Israelites. They were slaves in Egypt until God redeemed them, and then they were wayfarers, making their way to the Land of Promise. We too have been liberated from bondage to sin, and we are wayfarers. We are exiles from Eden who have heard the call to come out of Babylon, and we are now returning from exile. Our destination is the holy city, the New Jerusalem, coming down out of heaven from God (Rev. 21:10). We will dwell in the new and better Eden, the fulfillment of the Promised Land, the new heaven and new earth.

13

THE CHURCH'S PLOT TENSION AND ITS RESOLUTION

The Bible's story and symbolism teach the church to understand who she is, what she faces, and how she should live as she longs for the coming of her King and Lord.

This should be easy, right? What's difficult about being the bride and body of Christ? What's hard about being the family of God, the temple of the Holy Spirit?

Shouldn't this journey through these barren lands on our way to the new heaven and earth be something like a risk-free, safety-guaranteed expedition? Shouldn't it be something that's exciting, though like a roller coaster ride—scary, but safe?

Is that how your life feels? It might seem like that sometimes, perhaps when you reflect on your security in Christ and your certainty that God will overcome all his enemies. But I don't think life typically feels that way, even for those who meditate on God's Word day and night. And it's not just because we've somehow lost perspective and aren't thinking about it correctly. Consider the Psalms.

The authors of the Psalms sense that they are constantly in mortal danger. They're not talking like life's a no-risk roller coaster. Life really is dangerous. We really do love people. We really do fear that people we love will be hurt. We really do face temptations. We've seen people we thought were holy have moral failures and make shipwreck of the faith—people we thought were pillars of the church. We've seen marriages of more than fifty years end in divorce.

Do you feel the tension in the church's plot? The church's story is that Christ has died as the Passover Lamb, liberating believers from slavery to sin. After the Passover, Moses led Israel to Mount Sinai, where the people received the law and the covenant. Christ is our new Moses who has given us a new and better law as part of a new and better covenant. Israel traveled through the wilderness to the Land of Promise. We are now traveling through this world on the way to a new and better Land of Promise, the new heaven and earth. Once in the land, David reigned over Israel as king. Jesus, our new and better David, is our King, and he will reign in justice and righteousness and never fail us.

Still, we know the church's plot is full of tension because we live that tension. We feel our worries, our burdens, and our enmities. But God has given us so many advantages that we should marvel that the author of the church's story is able to produce real, convincing tension in the plot of this story.

We saw that it was Satan's temptation of Adam and Eve, overcoming them when they sinned, that introduced tension into the Bible's big story. Though Satan has suffered a decisive defeat at the cross of Christ, he has not yet been removed to his eternal cage. He has been defeated, but he has not surrendered.

He has been driven from the heavenly field of battle, but he has come down to earth for a little time and is making war on the woman and on her seed (Rev. 12:7–17).

Why would God allow this? We may not be able to give a comprehensive answer to that question, but we know that God is allowing it. We also know that God is not surprised by it. It's not as though Satan has gotten the better of God by avoiding capture.

How do we know that? Because this time of affliction for God's people was prophesied in the Old Testament. Daniel 7:23–25 depicts a satanic persecution of the people of God before God's people receive the kingdom described in 7:26–27. Daniel 12:7 speaks of "the shattering of the power of the holy people" coming to an end before all things are accomplished.

The picture we're given of the end parallels what we see at the cross: Satan thought he had defeated God when the Messiah was crucified, but God accomplished victory through what looked like defeat. Now, the people of the Messiah will conquer the same way that Jesus did: by being faithful unto death in the face of satanic opposition.

Satan is not trying a new strategy against the church. He is pursuing the same strategy he pursued against the Messiah. Satan is trying to destroy the church the same way he tried to destroy Jesus. God will get glory over Satan as the church is faithful unto death the same way he got glory over Satan as Jesus conquered by being faithful unto death.

This is why the New Testament has so much to say about tribulation and affliction. Satan is trying to destroy the church with these afflictions and tribulations. Through these same tribulations and afflictions, God is showing his power in the church's weakness. This is why Paul went around telling the churches that "through many tribulations we must enter the kingdom of God" (Acts 14:22).

The suffering of the Messiah and the people of the Messiah is sometimes referred to as the messianic woes. If you're a believer in Jesus, you're the bride and body of Christ, you're a part of the family of God, you're the temple of the Holy Spirit, and—surprising as it may seem—your life is going to be *hard*, not easy, because you will not avoid the messianic woes. If it was necessary for the Messiah first to suffer and then to enter into his glory (Luke 24:26), it is also necessary for the church to go through many tribulations and then to enter the kingdom (Acts 14:22).

Ironically, the only way to avoid the tribulations and afflictions is to join the losing team. Join Satan against God, and the messianic woes won't be yours. Instead, you'll have worldliness. But you'll find that worldliness doesn't satisfy your soul. You'll find that the lust of the eyes, the lust of the flesh, and the pride of life leave your mouth dry, your throat parched, and gravel in your gut. You'll find your life ruined by the fleeting pleasures of sin.

But if you trust in Jesus, repent of sin, and walk with him through the messianic woes, you'll find that he is with you when you pass through fire (Isa. 43:2). You'll find that when there seems to be no hope, the dawn breaks and the Savior comes. You'll find that your brokenness is an opportunity for him to show his healing power. You'll find that when you are exhausted is when he bears you up on eagle's wings as you hope in him.

You'll find what Paul found (cf. 2 Cor. 6:8–10):

- though the world treats you as an imposter, you're true;
- though you are unknown in the eyes of the world, you are known to the one whose opinion matters;
- though you die, you will live;
- though you feel deep sorrow, you are always rejoicing;
- though you are poor, you make many rich;
- though you have nothing, you possess everything.

You'll find that though the messianic woes turn your life into ashes, God makes them beautiful and gives you strength in place of tears (Isa. 61:3). The weeping will last the night; the joy will come in the morning (Ps. 30:5).

The Bible's story and symbolism teach the church to understand who she is, what she faces, and how she should live as she longs for the coming of her King and Lord. We are to follow Jesus, being faithful unto death, loving God and neighbor, laying down our lives for others as he laid down his for us.

Make no mistake about it: people all around us are living their lives in light of a larger story. For many, the story that explains their lives is a cheap satanic imitation of the true story of the world. This is why they hope some politician will be their messiah. This is why they hope that medicine will give eternal life, why they look to evolution as their creation myth, and hope to "change the world" into kingdom come now by means of political machinations, judicial rulings, or legislative triumphs.

I am not taking anything away from seeking to do all we can for God's glory and the good of others. I am simply asserting that we were made to live in the true story, not some fictional imitation of it with its shamans or scientists, priests or pundits, prophets or politicians.

God's name will be hallowed. God's kingdom will come. God's will indeed will be done, on earth as in heaven. That's the story the Bible is telling.

What will it be like when God finally redeems his people? It will be like the wedding day. The bride will have made herself ready with righteous deeds, which are the fine white linen bridal gown (Rev. 19:6–8). And the Bridegroom like no other will come (Rev. 19:11–16).

Battle won.
War over.
Victory complete.
Suffering fulfilled.

Woes accomplished.
Promises kept.
Lovers faithful.
Joy eternal.

Hope realized.
Faith sight.
Kingdom come.
Name hallowed.

EPILOGUE

Biblical theology is an attempt to get out of this world into another. We might call it a bridge; we might call it a rocket. The point is that we're trying to get our minds and hearts out of worldliness and into the Bible's symbolic universe.

Caution: don't think that studying biblical theology is going to do this for you. The best way to learn biblical theology, the best way to get yourself out of the world's way of thinking and into the Bible's *is to study the Bible itself.* Don't make this harder than it needs to be. Read the Bible. A lot.

I've found that the best way for me to see the interconnectedness of the Bible is to read big chunks of the Bible at one sitting. Instead of reading the Bible in little bits, why not sit down and read as much of Genesis as you can at one time? Really give yourself to the study of the Bible. Take a week and try to read the whole Old Testament straight through. It would take the whole week and more, but can you think of a better way to spend a week?

As I read the Bible in big chunks, I learn most if I mark connections between chapters or books or authors with colored pencils. That way I can find that quotation of Deuteronomy 4:29 in Jeremiah 29:13, for example.

Another thing that has helped me tremendously has been taking a guided tour of the Bible led by a book on biblical theology. My understanding of the Old Testament was enriched by reading Paul House's *Old Testament Theology* alongside my reading of the Old Testament itself. I would let House introduce a section of, say, Genesis to me, and then I would go read that portion of Genesis. My book *God's Glory in Salvation through Judgment: A Biblical Theology*, goes book-by-book through the whole Bible, and a great way to use it would be to read that book alongside your regular Bible reading.

If you're interested in pursuing biblical theology further, what follows is a short list of books on this topic you might turn to next.

FOR FURTHER READING

WHOLE-BIBLE BIBLICAL THEOLOGIES

Hamilton, James M., Jr. *God's Glory in Salvation through Judgment: A Biblical Theology*. Wheaton, IL: Crossway, 2010.

Gentry, Peter, and Stephen Wellum. *Kingdom through Covenant: A Biblical-Theological Understanding of the Covenants*. Wheaton, IL: Crossway, 2012.

Schreiner, Thomas R. *The King in His Beauty: A Biblical Theology of the Old and New Testaments*. Grand Rapids: Baker, 2013.

OLD TESTAMENT THEOLOGIES

House, Paul R. *Old Testament Theology*. Downers Grove, IL: InterVarsity, 1998.

Dempster, Stephen G. *Dominion and Dynasty: A Biblical Theology of the Hebrew Bible*. New Studies in Biblical Theology. Downers Grove, IL: InterVarsity, 2003.

NEW TESTAMENT THEOLOGIES

Ladd, George Eldon. *A Theology of the New Testament*. Edited by Donald Hagner. Rev. ed. Grand Rapids: Eerdmans, 1993.

Thielman, Frank. *Theology of the New Testament: A Canonical and Synthetic Approach*. Grand Rapids: Zondervan, 2005.

Schreiner, Thomas R. *New Testament Theology: Magnifying God in Christ*. Grand Rapids: Baker, 2008.

Beale, G. K. *A New Testament Biblical Theology: The Transformation of the Old Testament in the New*. Grand Rapids: Baker, 2011.

BOOKS ON THE TOPIC OF BIBLICAL THEOLOGY

Alexander, T. D., Brian S. Rosner, Graeme Goldsworthy, and D. A. Carson, eds. *New Dictionary of Biblical Theology*. Downers Grove, IL: InterVarsity, 2000.

Goldsworthy, Graeme. *According to Plan: The Unfolding Revelation of God in the Bible*. Downers Grove, IL: InterVarsity, 2002.

Alexander, T. D. *From Eden to the New Jerusalem: Exploring God's Plan for Life on Earth*. Nottingham, UK: Inter-Varsity, 2008.

Lawrence, Michael. *Biblical Theology in the Life of the Church: A Guide for Ministry*. Wheaton, IL: Crossway, 2010.

ACKNOWLEDGMENTS

The trumpet will sound, the archangel give voice, the skies split, and he will come: King of kings, Lord of lords, David's heir, Lion of Judah, seed of the woman, Lamb standing as though slain, hope of the world, healer of the sick, raiser of the dead, consolation for every woe, joy of man's desiring, the one who is worthy of allegiance and praise, victor over death, author of faith, champion, Christ. On that day the kingdom of the world will become the kingdom of our Lord and of his Christ, and he shall reign forever. Cue *hallelujahs*.

The world that is to come will know no weapons or warfare, no hearts will cheat, no nations rage. Lions will eat straw like the ox and little children play by the hole of the cobra: nothing to fear, for the curse will be rolled back and the desert become like Eden land. The Bible's story arc lands in a new and better Eden, a new heaven and new earth, and we shall be like Jesus, for we shall see him as he is.

Psalm 1 describes the blessing of meditating on the Bible, and the poetry depicts delight in God's Word producing a person who is like a tree planted in the garden of the Lord. To be always mindful of the Word of the Lord is to be always mindful of the Lord himself. To be always mindful of the Lord is to walk with him, to abide in him, and wasn't that the best thing about Eden anyway? Thus biblical theology, which seeks to shape the mind according to the Scriptures to understand and embrace the worldview of the biblical authors as it is reflected in their writings, takes us out of this world into another. The world into which biblical theology takes us is the world that is to come.

Happy are the people whose God is the Lord, who have access to his Word, who meditate on it day and night, walking with him; for to abide in him turns the trackless waste into a garden in the cool of the day, as he himself becomes a booth for shade by day and a shelter from the wind and rain. There is no one like the Lord.

My praise and thanks, then, are to God the Father through Christ the Son by the power of the Holy Spirit. He has given us his Word, and what a gift it is. And he did not spare his own Son! Hand on mouth—what love. None greater. And life by the Spirit, and forgiveness in Christ, sweet and tender mercies, melt the heart of stone.

How can I thank the Lord for all his benefits to me? My wife is a wonder beyond words, and our children bring joys past all we could have imagined or hoped (sometimes consternations on the same order!). We are so thankful for the wider circle of people enjoying the foretaste of the world to come with us at Kenwood Baptist Church. God's Word is rich, the ordinances of baptism and the Lord's Supper thrill and sustain us, the musicians are skilled, and our hearts by grace are full of faith, hope, and love.

I dedicate this book to our daughter, Evie Caroline, with the prayer that biblical theology will take her all the way to the city that has foundations, whose architect and builder is God.

GENERAL INDEX

SCRIPTURE INDEX

Demonstrating the Glory of God in His Justice and Mercy

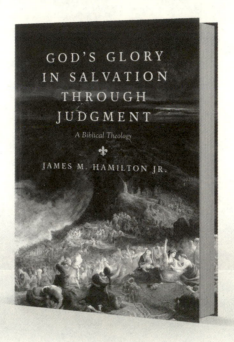